P9-DXD-387

THE
FABYOULIST

THE FAB**YOU**LIST

LIST IT, LIVE IT,
LOVE YOUR LIFE

SUSAN CAMPBELL CROSS

FEBRUARY BOOKS

Library of Congress Control Number: 2013938864
The FabYOUList
List It, Live It, Love Your Life
Susan Campbell Cross
p.cm.
1. Self-Help / Personal Growth / Happiness 2. Personal Growth 3. Memoirs
Susan Campbell Cross—1st Edition

ISBN-13: 978-0-9849543-4-6
ISBN-10: 0-9849543-4-1

Cover design by Veronica Zhu • Book design Casey Hampton

February Books
215 Park Avenue South
New York, NY 10003
www.februarybooks.com

Printed in the United States of America

CONTENTS

INTRODUCTION

For me the anxiety over turning forty started just after my thirty-sixth birthday, when I suddenly realized I was on the other side of thirty-five, closer to forty than thirty. It wasn't the number or the age that concerned me, it was the fact that I thought I would've done more, seen more, *become* more by the time I entered the middle years of my life. What exactly did I feel I would've done, seen, and become? I wasn't entirely sure. I just had an overwhelming sense that I had a lot of unfinished (un-started, actually) business to attend to, and less and less time in which to attend to it. With each tick of the clock I was closer to that "F bomb," *forty*.

Always a list maker, I took out a piece of paper and began to compose not a "to-do" list, but more of a "wish-I-had-done" list. Ironically, when I was finished there were forty things on it, the last of which was "write a book." By the way, this book you're holding in your hands right now, *is* that book. *The FabYOUList: List It, Live It, Love Your Life* chronicles my experiences as I set out to tackle numbers one through thirty-nine—all before my fortieth birthday. In living my list I embarked on a life-changing, eye-opening journey of self-discovery. And here I thought I was just going to do some cool stuff and, I hoped, have a little fun. I did do some cool stuff and it *was* fun, but it was so much more: without realizing it, I had come up with a concrete plan with which I would transform my life and become the person I always dreamed I would be, the person I was always meant to be, my true authentic self.

Before I made that list I was hard-pressed to answer the simple question, "Who are you?" I'd always answered in terms of who I was in relation to others: "I'm a mother, a wife, a daughter, a sister." The person I've become is a complete woman with goals and aspirations of her own, a sense of purpose, and dreams for the future. Not just dreams for those around her, but for herself. By the time I'd achieved everything on my list I was the version of myself I'd dreamed up as a child.

Remember when you were little and you used to think about what you'd be when you grew up? Are you doing that now or even a modified version? I know I wasn't. Early on I had aspirations of being a trapeze artist. Not that I want to do that now, but I needed to get in touch with that little girl who dreamed of it in the first place. Where did that girl go, the one who dreamed big and had no fear of failure? What happened to make her stop believing that she could be anything she wanted, could confidently leap off a platform and fly through the air effortlessly to the deafening applause of throngs of fans, taking her bow gracefully with deep satisfaction and gratitude, dazzling in the spotlight in head-to-toe sequins as if to say, "Here I am world! Aren't I *amazing*?"

When had I stopped dreaming dreams for myself and trying to make them come true? And perhaps more important, *why*? I had majored in writing and got a job in advertising fresh out of college, but I quit when my first born, Kayla, was an infant. There used to be all kinds of things I wanted to do and places I wanted to see, but I wasn't doing anything or going anywhere. Somehow over the years I had lost touch with what I wanted, who I was, how I felt, and I started doing what so many of us do: living for everyone else. It wasn't enough to approve of myself; I sought the approval of my parents, my teachers, and my peers. I did what was expected of me, always the good daughter, the good student, and the good friend. Later, I was the good wife and the good mother.

I met my husband, Kevin, at UC San Diego, when I was a sophomore and he was a junior. We got married a year after I graduated and started a family the year after that. We had three children in four and a half years, and my life became all about them. I'm not saying that's a bad thing—it's one of the things I am most proud of, being a mom. But I realize now that being a parent doesn't mean you can't have a life of your own as well. For years I hid behind my family, using them as an excuse not to try things.

I claimed that I didn't want to put myself out there, take chances, or pursue my dreams, because I was afraid I'd be taking time away from the kids. I did a good job convincing myself that this was the whole truth. But in taking on the challenge of fulfilling my list I discovered what the *real* obstacle was. Me. More accurately, me and my fear. My list was the key to getting out of my own way, kicking my fear to the curb, and replacing it with the courage I needed to live my life to its fullest, to be the best me possible. And you know what? The kids didn't suffer *at all*. They are better off because of it. I have come to realize the value of modeling for them how important it is to "go for it," no matter what your "it" is. In doing so I have become more than a good mother, wife, sister, daughter—I've become a complete individual person who is fulfilled, happy, confident, and fearless. And it all started with a list!

The more I shared my journey with people, the more I learned I wasn't alone. It seems that women, especially, although certainly not exclusively, tend to let pieces of themselves fade for one reason or another. Have you ever gotten so lost in your role of caregiver that you've willingly pushed yourself to the back burner if not off of the stove entirely? Do you feel guilty and selfish every time you stop to take care of yourself? Do you worry that if you do, your family will somehow suffer from it? Do you feel like you aren't worthy of the attention and time it would take to achieve your own dreams? Are you worried that should you try, you might fail? If any of this sounds familiar, then this book was written for just for you, in the hope that you will embark on a journey of your own, a journey that will lead to a happier, healthier, more fulfilled YOU.

So now you know all about my midlife panic attack, and my subsequent list. Here's the part where I tell you what's on it. So, without further ado, ladies and gentlemen (DRUM ROLL PLEASE): my list.

1. Get Googleable
2. Have an article published
3. Invite someone to lunch whom I admire, but don't know well
4. Run a 5k
5. Get involved with a cause I believe in
6. Do a charity project with the kids
7. Take an adult ballet class
8. Fly on the trapeze
9. Try yoga at ~~the beach~~ the rec center
10. Go church shopping (pick a religion, any religion)
11. Do something to honor my parents
12. Do something to honor my grandparents
13. Perform on stage in a play or musical
14. Take guitar lessons

15. Get a paid acting job
16. Get to know the neighbors
17. Start a neighborhood tradition
18. Ride my bike
19. Play bitch's bingo
20. Sunbathe topless
21. Crash a party
22. Go clubbing VIP-style in Vegas
23. Go to a strip club
24. Go skinny-dipping
25. Drive an ATV
26. Go whitewater rafting
27. Go zip-lining
28. Learn to surf
29. Get back on a horse
30. Have a completely organized closet
31. Get my passport stamped
32. Plan a girls' getaway weekend
33. Go wine tasting
34. Take the boys camping
35. Travel somewhere alone
36. Watch some of the old classic movies (the "must-sees" I haven't seen)
37. Be a sports fan
38. Go paddle boarding
39. Go au naturel for a week
40. Write a book

So that's my list. There may be a few things on it that made you laugh, or scratch your head, or blush even, but that's okay because my list is about me. Everything on it is significant to me and was some-thing I truly wanted to accomplish. I came up with those particular things by asking myself some questions, doing some soul searching, revisiting a few childhood memories, and letting myself imagine what my life might look like if I were the one designing it, which it turns out, I am.

The last and most rewarding challenge on my list was to write a book, *this* book, which I hope will encourage people to make a list of their own, embrace life more fully, and discover their best and most authentic self. It's a method that worked for me, and I'm positive it will work for you, too. You know how I know that? Because your list will be about you; it's not a one-size-fits-all type of thing.

Whether you are approaching a milestone birthday as I was, or just want to kick-start your life, I urge you to carve out some quiet time and make a list of your own. If you feel as I did, that there were things you wanted to do or should have done, and you are having difficulty figuring out exactly what those things are, you might try asking yourself a few questions:

1. When you were a child, what did you want to be when you grew up?
2. What you would be doing if you knew that you couldn't fail?
3. Do you have a project started that is sitting somewhere unfinished?
4. Are you afraid of something, anything, but wish you weren't?

These questions will lead to some interesting answers, and those answers will lead to the discovery of what should go on your list. Don't worry about what you put down so much as whether or not it's something specific to you and your life. I can't tell you how many times people wanted to offer me suggestions. "Why not skydiving?" one well-intentioned friend asked. The more pertinent question was, "*Why* skydiving?" I couldn't come up with a really good answer for that, which told me that it had no place on my list. The fact that it was something my friend had always wanted to try was a big hint that it belonged on *her* list, which I hope is where she put it. The point is that my list had to be about me, just as your list has to be about you.

As you draw up your list, don't be afraid to edit. There were things on my initial list that got modified or scratched off entirely once I took the time to really think through how important they were to me. You don't have to come up with any specific number of things either. Do ten things, twenty things, *one hundred* things; it's entirely up to you. And while I do think it's good to give yourself a deadline of sorts, I don't think that it ultimately matters if you complete everything by that date. Spoiler alert: I did NOT finish my list before my fortieth! The important thing is to get motivated and set the wheels in motion. Make a list, check it twice (or three or four times)—and think of it not as a "to-do" list but as a set of step-by-step instructions for building a better life.

ONE THING LEADS TO ANOTHER

When I turned thirty-six I had a stunning realization. I wasn't just thirty-six, I was pushing forty. And I was freaking out. Something was missing. But what? Here I had this beautiful family, a husband who loved me no matter what, and three healthy children. Still, I felt restless and incomplete. What was it that was troubling me? It wasn't my age. I knew thirty-six wasn't exactly old. The more I thought about it, the more I realized it was the fact that I had reached the middle years of my life and what had I really accomplished, aside from having kids? Not much. When I was younger I had hopes and dreams and aspirations, but once I became a mother, I lost track of all of that. Moms tend to do that, it's part of the job description to put our children's needs before our own. Up until that fateful birthday freak-out, though, putting their needs before mine meant ignoring mine almost entirely. I had to do something about it.

I've always been a big fan of the to-do list. If I don't write things down, I tend to forget about them. (I call it *momnesia*.) My lists were always full of mundane tasks such as grocery shopping, picking up the dry cleaning, and taking my kids to their eight hundred activities. I made a new to-do list every day, but I never put myself on it. I decided to make a different sort of list. One that was entirely about me and things I wanted to do for myself, not just things I had to do for everybody else. It took me quite a long time to do it, too, evidence of how long it had been since I'd given myself any real consideration. In the end I came up with forty challenges, some hard, some easy, some downright nutty. When I was finished, I had forty goals, and no clue how to go about accomplishing them. All of a sudden I felt overwhelmed. Forty things—that's alot. I hadn't done any of these things for the first thirty-six years of my life. Now I was challenging myself to do all of them before my fortieth.

The first thing I put on my list resulted from my having done what only the most insecure and vain people do: I Googled myself. I typed in my name, hit enter, waited the split second and . . . nada. I tried again with a different version of my name, and . . . zip. Zilch. Again and again, I typed in all different variations of my name. Susan Cross. Susan Campbell. Susan Campbell Cross. Susan Lee Cross. Susan Lee Campbell. Susan Lee Campbell Cross. Still nothing. This bothered me to no end. I wanted to be accomplished, to have done something important that would be recognized by others and searchable on the Internet. Like I said, I was insecure. I was looking for outside approval, as if my self worth depended on other people finding me worthy, worthy of mentioning on the Internet.

Being un-Googleable in L.A. is the equivalent of being untouchable in India. Was it possible that I'd done absolutely nothing of note in all my years on Earth? Somebody must have quoted me at some point or taken a photo and listed me in the caption. Sure, I'd been somewhat isolated since having the kids, but I wasn't invisible, was I? I'd taught a summer of Sunday school (this was during my Presbyterian phase). I'd attended a party for a famous fashion designer (I'm friends with his twin sister), and I knew someone had snapped a photo or two of me there. I thought for sure there would be some mention of me somewhere out there in the wide world of cyberspace. I'd hoped to find some sign that maybe I wasn't as unaccomplished as I'd thought, that perhaps I'd done something interesting or impactful (aside from raising the kids, I mean) and somehow forgotten about it. But, after all my searches I had to accept the cold hard truth. I was un-Googleable.

Changing this sad fact became the number one goal on my list. How was I supposed to find myself if I couldn't even search myself? I was determined to transform myself from un-Googleable to Google-worthy. But, *how*? I live in L.A., I thought. I could go pantyless to all the hot clubs and flash the paparazzi and then feign ignorance. Nope. That'd been done. Thanks alot, Britney, Paris, Lindsay, et al. I could come up with an amazing invention and market it, becoming one of the ten richest women in the world. But that would require me to come up with an amazing invention. I could commit some random crime, say rob a GAP Kids or something, and then bribe the cops to leak my mug shot to the press. But if I did that, I'd most likely get sent to prison and lord knows the orange jumpsuits and fluorescent lighting are really unflattering. What could I do . . . what could I do?

All that thinking made me hungry, so I decided to go to a nearby shopping center for a quick bite. Maybe something would come to me once my stomach was full. This was right in the middle of the busy lunch hour and the parking lot was crowded. I managed to get a spot just a tad closer than Egypt and started walking toward the restaurant. I had to pass a few stores on my way, one of which was Barnes & Noble. I don't know what possessed me to go inside—I was really hungry and could smell the fresh bread from the restaurant—

but in I went and there on one of the tables was a sign from God. Moses had his burning bush and I had my glossy-white paperback entitled, *The Huffington Post Complete Guide to Blogging*.

I swear I heard angels singing and harps playing as I paid in cash and then practically sprinted to the restaurant. I sat there for well over an hour, much to the waitress's dismay, completely engrossed as I read about how to create a blog. It turns out there are a lot of sites that host bloggers for free, one of which (there were those angels and harps again) was Google. If I posted a blog on Google's site, "Blogspot," and if I entered in key words that would come up when people searched Google using those words, I would finally be, and I dared to believe it . . . Googleable.

One of the many pieces of advice in that book was to blog about what you know—write from your own experience. The problem was if I'd had an experience interesting enough to blog about, I probably would have been Googleable a long time ago. Still, I decided to give it a go. I titled my blog *Secrets of a Suburban Soccer Mom* and wrote a post about the decision to have a third child, *Third Time's the Charm*. When I finished, I clicked "publish post" and then proceeded to check for comments every five minutes for the next few days. I also tried Googling myself again and again, hoping to find myself.

I wrote another post, *Does This Sound Familiar?* about what I like to refer to as "overactivityitis," the disease that is spreading rampantly through suburbia causing formerly sane parents to sign up for an outrageous number of sports, play groups, and classes which in turn causes kids to be rushed from thing to thing to thing. The driving and the fast food and the lack of downtime had really affected my life. And you know what? I wasn't the only one. I began to get a few comments and was encouraged to write again. I'd just been on a field trip to the zoo with my son's fourth grade class and had gotten lost. The teacher and I were separated from the group for the longest forty-five minutes of my life, during which we walked in circles trying to find the kids and the poor lonely mother who'd been left to wrangle all of them in our absence. People found my trauma amusing. And so I wrote again. I had so much fun writing that I forgot to check my status on the Internet. After a week or so into my new life as a blogger, I tried one more time. I went to Google search, cautiously typed "Susan Campbell Cross," and clicked "Enter." Eureka.

#1 ~~Get Googleable~~

. . . .

By the time I'd rendered myself Googleable I no longer cared. If you believe that one, I have a bridge in Brooklyn you might be interested in. Of course I still cared! I was elated I was now findable on the Internet. But my happiness wasn't just about the ends; the means were just as rewarding. I'd found real purpose in blogging. I was doing something I loved (writing) and was getting some very positive feedback for it. Some of my kids' friends were even reading my blog. This, of course, had the added benefit of leverage. Any time one of my kids started to act up I'd say, "Go right ahead. All you're doing is giving me more material for my blog." That was one threat they knew I'd follow through with. I suddenly had a new appreciation for the saying "The pen is mightier than the sword." Or in this case, blogging is mightier than grounding.

Blogging, I discovered, was mightier than a lot of things. Mighty enough, in fact, to be the means by which I accomplished another of the goals from my list, "Have an article published." I suppose that every post I wrote for the blog could be considered an article published, but I wasn't counting them since I was the one who had published them. Then I got an e-mail from a travel website saying they'd *re*published a post I'd written about a vacation I'd taken with my husband. They liked me! They really, really liked me! They liked

me so much that they'd taken something I'd written without permission and republished it! Wait a minute. Should I have been flattered or outraged? Who cares?! They liked me! Moreover, they
wanted to know if I'd consider writing more travel articles for them
to steal. Steal, publish—six of one, half-dozen of the other.

I couldn't have been happier. I'd crossed another goal off of my
list and it had taken no effort at all. A short while later I got a couple
more e-mails, one from an online social networking site that catered
to families and one for a parenting eZine (online magazine), both
asking me to be a contributor. In the words of that ever-so-
philosophical eighties band The Fixx, "One thing (yeah, one thing)
leads to another."

#2 ~~Have an article published~~

. . . .

The one thing leads to another phenomenon didn't end there. It
seemed to happen quite often, actually—where going after one goal
was like knocking down the first in a line of dominos. Here's another example. I had put "invite someone to lunch whom I admire
but don't know well" on my list. I thought it would be a great learning experience for me to talk to a person who had achieved something I aspired to achieve myself. I realize that to most people inviting
someone to lunch is a simple task, but for me it was daunting. I felt
more than a little bit silly calling an individual I barely knew, let
alone asking her to eat lunch with me. I mean, there were a million
reasons I'd like to sit and talk with *her*. But what reason could she
possibly have to want to sit and talk with *me*?

Who *was* this person, a woman I was worried wouldn't even re-
member me, let alone want to spend some of her time with me?
Nancy Alspaugh. Nancy lived in my neighborhood (still does), and
I'd met her once at a mutual friend's fundraising boutique, but I'd

known who she was long before that. I'd seen her name on an invitation I'd received for Denim & Diamonds, an annual event benefitting Act Today!, an organization that provides grants to families with autistic children. She was listed as the organization's executive director. Some of her many other accomplishments were listed, too: author, playwright, and television producer.

To say I was impressed would be a gross understatement. Nancy was doing everything I'd dreamed of doing. She'd had a high-power, high-profile career in the entertainment industry, had performed on stage, was a published author, and upon learning that her son Wyatt had autism had the courage and strength to take on the huge task of running ACT Today! What had I been doing? A whole lot of dreaming and not a lot of doing, that's what. So why on earth would Nancy Alspaugh want to go to lunch with me? I was very sure she wouldn't. I was also fairly certain she wouldn't know who I was when I called. I was wrong.

Turns out Nancy knew exactly who I was, and she seemed to be genuinely happy to hear from me. Of course, the little negative voice in my head reminded me that Nancy was a pretty good actor, so maybe she was only *acting* like she remembered me and *acting* as though she were happy to talk to me. But for once in my life I decided to turn that little negative voice down long enough to hear what someone else had to say. Nancy said she would be happy to meet me for lunch, and when would I like to go?

We made a plan to meet the following week at the Corner Bakery. When the day arrived, I was really nervous. I must have changed my outfit five times. I wanted to look nice, but at the same time, I didn't want to appear too eager. Who was I fooling? I was *extremely* eager. I wanted to know everything about this woman. The bio info from the Denim & Diamonds invitation was just the tip of the iceberg. Thank God for that! If I'd known exactly how amazing Nancy was, I might have chickened out of making that call.

She'd produced several shows for television, had produced Matt Lauer before she married him (and yes, I'm talking about *that* Matt Lauer, of the *Today* show), she'd been a teenage groupie of Bruce Springsteen (so, of course, that means she knows him personally); she'd co-written and co-starred in a two-woman stage production called *Boomer Babes*; she'd penned two books for grown-ups and one for children; she'd produced a documentary about a drug addict; married her second husband, Read Jackson, who was an executive producer at Fox Sports; adopted a son, found out he had autism, and became the director for *ACT Today!* And oh, she had also recently completed a marathon—just for kicks. I was exhausted just listening to her. Exhausted and extremely impressed. What else can I say? This woman rocks. And I hoped some of it might rub off on me.

I mustered the courage to tell her that I'd invited her to lunch as part of a project. I explained my midlife freak-out, my subsequent list, and my mission to cross everything off of it before I turned forty. At the risk of sounding like a stalker, I admitted our lunch date was #3. "What a terrific idea!" she said. "You know, this would really resonate with a lot of women. You could write this as a one-woman show. You would be the star. I can *totally* see that. Or a reality TV show! This would make great TV. I know someone who produces reality shows. That would be a lot of fun to watch—women setting out to fulfill their dreams, figuring some things out about themselves." Nancy was in high producer mode, and I hoped my jaw hadn't dropped, because I was completely and utterly floored.

Not only did this woman whom I held in such high regard think I had a good idea, she thought I could really do something with it; in helping myself, I could help others. Suddenly I wasn't some inexperienced peon, I was someone who had a great idea, the courage to conquer new-things, and the talent to parlay it into various different mediums. This was all heady stuff. "I wouldn't know where to begin with all of that—but it all sounds wonderful to me!" I said. "Right now I'm just working on my list."

"Darling," Nancy grabbed my hands and looked at me intensely, "I'm going to tell you something very important so I want you to listen carefully. In this world you can accomplish anything, *anything* at all. You just have to know people. And honey," she squeezed my hands hard to really drive this point home, "You know people." And after that lunch, I truly did.

Nancy is a problem solver. It's the producer in her, I suppose. I started giving her the rundown of some of the other things on my list. When I got to, "Run a 5k" and "Get involved with a cause I believe in," she clapped her hands excitedly. "PERFECT! You can do 'Wyatt's Run' (named for her son), and you can get involved with ACT Today! *Done* and *done!*"

I learned a lot from my "take someone to lunch" challenge, perhaps most important, not to listen to that little negative voice in my head. If I had, I never would have had lunch with Nancy. And, if I hadn't had lunch with Nancy I wouldn't have had a lead on two of my other goals. In other words, those dominos would still be standing. Another thing I learned is that seeking out the advice of someone who has accomplished something you're trying to do is really smart. I believe my IQ went up a few points after that lunch date, and I'm positive that my confidence level did. Nancy's enthusiasm added fuel to my own. I left feeling as if I could take on the world, and if I could do that, a few dozen or so challenges should be a piece of cake.

#3 Invite someone to lunch whom I admire but don't know well

. . . .

If you look at your list and start feeling as overwhelmed as I did, try focusing on just one goal. Chances are, as you work on conquering one, opportunities to achieve others will appear as if by magic. The key is to share with others what your goals are. Seek out people who are knowledgeable in areas related to your list. Be proactive in asking for advice (and in following it) and keep your eyes open for new opportunities. One thing really does lead to another, and another, and another.

TWO

SWEET CHARITY

Wyatt's Run, the race Nancy had told me about, consisted of ultra-marathon runner Shannon Farar-Griefer running twenty-four hours straight on dirt trails that lace through Ahmanson Ranch, an area that's officially known as the Upper Las Virgenes Canyon Open Space Preserve (but let's face it—that's way too much of a mouthful). Anyway, anyone else who wanted to participate in the race could either sponsor Shannon or get his own sponsors and run himself (or herself in my case). I could get my 5k run accomplished and get involved in a cause I believed in all at the same time. Kill two birds with one stone. Not that I'm into killing birds, or anything, but you get the picture.

The only thing was Wyatt's Run wasn't a 5k; it had a five-mile course and a ten-mile course. Now, I am far from a math person let alone a metric system person, but I had a pretty good idea that five miles was farther than five kilometers. I wasn't in terrible shape, I did go to kickboxing three times a week, and lifted weights, too. Could I pull off a five-mile race? There was only one way to find out. So, with the race only a couple of weeks away, I started collecting sponsors and RSVP'd to the kick-off party for the event. There was no turning back.

After our lunch, Nancy and I became very good friends. She invited me to go running with her Hidden Hills running group—the group who'd run the L.A. Marathon with her—the group who is trained by Shannon Farar-Griefer, that crazy ultra-marathoner I mentioned earlier. They normally run in Ahmanson Ranch on the exact trails that we'd be running on the day of the race. I figured it would be a good idea for me to know what I was getting myself into, so I met up with them early one morning. Prior to that I'd taken a test run by myself from my house to the other side of Hidden Hills and back, a distance that, according to my car odometer, was five miles. But I quickly learned that five miles on pavement was not at all the same as five miles on steep, uneven dirt trails. There was one spot where we had to cross a creek on a wet mossy log. I hadn't faced anything like that jogging along the street.

Even though these ladies had been doing this six times a week since forever, I was determined to keep up or at least not fall too far behind, or into the creek for that matter. Every once in a while their fearless leader Shannon stopped and waited for me to catch up. "Are you okay?" she'd ask.

"Yes," I'd answer, but seriously, I wasn't too sure.

"Well, you're still talking," Shannon reasoned, "That means you can keep running." And so I did. I had no idea how far, though, because Shannon refused to tell me. "I never say until we're done," she said with a smile. Bitch. When we finally were done, I was absolutely spent.

"Do you think that if I do this a few more times I'll be able to run the five-mile loop for Wyatt's Run?" I panted.

"Five miles?" Shannon laughed. "You just ran nine."

I didn't know I had that in me, but somehow Shannon and the other ladies did. Those amazing, beautiful, intelligent, determined, accomplished women, who were not only marathon runners, but also mothers, charity directors, writers, real estate agents, producers, clothing designers, event planners, and media mavens thought that I had it in me. *Me*, I thought, the one who was worried about being able to run a five-mile race. These ladies saw my five miles and raised me five more. I decided that I would run the ten-mile course at Wyatt's Run. And because they had faith in me, I found a new faith in myself. It seemed that the annoyingly negative voice in my head, the one that did indeed turn out to be my own, was now singing a new tune. *YES YOU CAN!* By surrounding myself with people who not only saw me, but who also saw all the potential within me, I began to see it, too. One thing leads to another after all.

And so I set out on the day of Wyatt's run in great spirits. I was happy to be running for a cause I believed in, to be running at all, actually. Until then I'd joked that I only ran when chased. But at the start of the race I was feeling pretty confident. There was just one thing that came up: I'd planned on it being tough; I'd planned on it being hot; I'd planned on being exhausted; I had not, however, planned on getting lost.

As I said, there were two courses. At the start, I was mixed in with a bunch of people, including a darling group of 'tweens who were running five miles. Then the trail split, and I said good-bye to them as they veered off onto their course and I veered off onto what I believed to be the ten-mile one. And at first I was going the right way; I was certain of it. But then I came to a fork and could have gone left or right. I picked right. And as you've probably figured out by now, I should have picked left.

By then it was over a hundred degrees and I was halfway through the water I'd brought. I thought I had five miles to go, but boy, was

I in for a surprise. As it turns out, I was running away from the course, and I kept on going. I didn't see any other runners for quite some time. I tried not to be worried about that—after all, I'd hung back with the five milers for so long, perhaps the ten milers had too much of a lead for me to catch up to them. I turned up my music and focused on the beauty of Ahmanson Ranch and not on the fact that it was home to rattlesnakes, coyotes, and mountain lions. After an hour or so, I turned my music off so that I could hear any noises the rattle snakes, coyotes, and mountain lions might have been making. I didn't want to be paranoid, but I also didn't want to be eaten alive. Every once in while my running would startle some unseen creature in the brush, and I would jump at the sound of their scurrying feet.

This went on for what seemed like an eternity. By then I was almost out of water and the sun was straight up and blazing in the cloudless sky. I was lost. Completely and utterly lost. It took all I had left not to cry. I was determined that if I were to get dehydrated, it would *not* be from crying. All of the emotion that I refused to let come out my eyes balled up in my throat, instead, causing a tremendous ache. I decided it might be better to slow to a walk—I didn't want my running to attract the attention of a mountain lion. I also decided to turn around. I'd been going the wrong direction and there seemed to be no end to the trail I was on. Perhaps it would be better to double back and see if that would lead me to the starting point of the race. But as I headed the other way, I saw forks in the path that I didn't recognize. Had I come from the left or the right? I honestly didn't know. I ran up hills, down hills, and on paths that were wide and looked more traveled and therefore more promising, that suddenly turned narrow and overgrown with brush.

"Hot out, isn't it?" Came a voice from up ahead. Finally! Husband-and-wife hikers who were insane enough to brave the midday heat were heading my way. Only problem was I couldn't answer them. My voice was lost inside that aching ball in my throat. I couldn't force a sound out no matter how hard I tried so I just nodded my head. "Are you all right? You aren't lost or anything are you?" the husband hiker asked. I nodded my head again. "Well, don't feel bad, you're the second runner we've found lost out here this week." I wasn't sure if he was just trying to make me feel better, or if perhaps I wasn't the only human being born completely void of any sense of direction. "We'll get you out if you want." Boy did I want. I nodded with relief and continued to nod as the woman tried to make conversation.

Eventually my voice returned and I told them where I lived and how truly grateful I was that they were willing to help me get home. I'd walked to the start of the race, which was at an entrance into the Ranch, about a mile or so from my house. "Wow—how'd you end up over here?" The wife asked.

"Over where?" I was still very disoriented. She pulled out a map and showed me where they'd parked their truck—at a different entrance way on the other side of the preserve and nowhere near my house or my neighborhood. We started trying to retrace my path. With all the circling back I had done we figured I had traveled about eighteen miles. So much for the 5k I'd put on my list. Once home I shed my sweat-soaked clothes, unlaced my dirt-caked running shoes, and peeled back my filthy socks. They were soaked through with sweat and blood and covered with foxtails. Then I saw my feet. I had two gnarly blisters, and I'd lost most of the toenail on the big toe on my left foot. Pretty. I stepped into the shower and stood under the cold water. I was embarrassed for having gotten lost. I was also beyond disappointed that I didn't finish the race. But then I thought about the money I'd raised for ACT Today! and how many miles I'd actually gone. I also felt pretty proud of myself for being able to keep my wits about me and not cry my way to dehydration or give up trying to find a way out of there.

I had learned a few things that day: 1) it's best to run with a buddy, 2) it's not a good idea to run in high heat, and 3) I have a terrible sense of direction. I have *no* sense of direction, and therefore shouldn't be out running without a cell phone or a GPS. Either that or someone should wire me with LoJack. I also learned that I'm stronger than I ever dreamed possible; that I'm smart enough to know when to walk to conserve energy and avoid mountain lions and stubborn enough to face my fear and overcome it. I hated being lost. But I loved finding myself.

#4 Run a 5k

#5 Get involved with a cause I believe in

· · · ·

I also really loved feeling that I'd done something to help others. "Get involved in a cause I believe in" wasn't the only philanthropic challenge on my list. I had also put down "do a charity project with the kids." This was something I'd wanted to do for quite some time. In fact, my daughter and I had already taken a stab at doing some good deeds together. We'd been recruited by a national organization that, in the interest of discretion and of not being sued, I'll simply call the "Charitable Ladies' League," CLL for short. I had a couple of friends who'd been involved with the CLL and both had called me during their membership drive saying how perfect Kayla and I would fit in.

Not just *anybody* could apply to be a member of the CLL. Oh no. You had to be sponsored and cosponsored by two members in good standing, and there was a whole lot of paperwork involved. They asked questions about our family, my employment history, my daughter's and my past experience doing community service, and my sorority affiliations. I was a Tri Delta in college—had been an officer every quarter. Also I was on the Panhellenic Council and had been inducted into the Order of Omega, a Greek honor society. So on paper, I must have looked really good. We were invited to attend the orientation meeting to determine whether or not we'd like to become "provisional" members.

On the day of the meeting they separated the daughters from the mothers and had us all rotate through various groups led by active members. Each group focused on a different aspect of the CLL, many of them, I noticed, had absolutely nothing to do with charity. They did, however, have to do with manners, etiquette, and dress codes. There were many rules one had to abide by if one was going to do charity as a member of the CLL. One rule that really stuck out concerned pantyhose. As in, you had to wear them. Not all the time, but enough of the time that it was going to suck.

Now, I should stop right here and say that my daughter, who is wonderful, is a tomboy. She never much cared for wearing dresses, and after her first grade holiday pageant I stopped trying to make her. The flyer the teacher had sent home said that boys were to wear jackets and ties, and girls should be in holiday dresses. I had purchased the poofiest confection I could find and laid it out on Kayla's bed with tights and a pair of patent-leather Mary Janes. She came down "ready to go" in a velour leopard-print pantsuit, uneven pigtails sprouting from either side of her head, and what can best be described as combat boots.

I thought she looked darling but reminded her of the dress code. She began to cry, wailing that I didn't like her because she didn't want to wear a dress. I told her I loved her no matter what she wore, that if she was comfortable with what she had on and didn't have a problem with being the only girl wearing pants, then I didn't have one either. She was the cutest thing up there, and while all the other girls looked like the cast of *Toddlers & Tiaras*, Kayla looked like Kayla with a smile from ear to ear. After that, we took every last dress out of her closet and gave them all away. I figured one day she might change her mind and we'd buy some new dresses. At the time of the CLL orientation Kayla was fourteen and that day had not yet come.

I was pretty sure that the mandatory wearing of pantyhose would be a deal breaker. I was secretly hoping it would be, because I was getting the feeling this group was of the twin-sweater-set and pearls-wearing variety. This is how I describe a certain type of woman who—how shall I put this politely—believe it's still 1952. Yes, that about sums it up. Pastel twin sweater sets, sensible shoes, slacks or smart little Ann Taylor skirts (nothing too short mind you), Laura Bush–like hairdos, pearls, and, of course, pantyhose.

I myself have never been a fan. I don't like the feeling of having my legs encased like sausages in those slippery nylon prisons. I was sure my daughter wouldn't want anything to do with the CLL after I let her in on the whole hose thing. Still, I wanted it to be her decision. So, on the way home from the orientation meeting I said nonchalantly, "What'd you think?"

"Good, I guess. Some of the girls were nice. Some were sort of cliquey." Thank God, I thought.

"They mentioned to us moms that sometimes we'll have to get pretty dressed up."

"Yeah, bummer," Kayla rolled her eyes. "I guess I can deal with it." Uh oh.

"We'll even have to wear . . . pantyhose," I said and held my breath.

"What are pantyhose?" This was going to be harder than I thought.

"They're like tights, only *worse*." I said making a gagging sound for effect.

"Oh. Well, that's okay I guess." What? She was okay with it? I was done for. If Kayla were willing to suck it up and wear hose, I'd have to do it, too. Great. Just great.

The Charitable Ladies' League had a policy that everyone in it must volunteer. Well, duh. That was what we were there for, right? Only they weren't talking about the volunteer work we'd be doing for others. They were talking about the volunteer work we'd be doing for the CLL itself. Every member had to have a job, and there were many different ones to choose from. So many, in fact, that there was a meeting just for the choosing of jobs. Meetings were very important to the CLL. If you had to miss one for any reason, you would be punished. The punishment was that you have to do extra volunteer work.

This hardly sounded like a punishment since the sole purpose of joining the CLL was to do volunteer work in the first place. But, as I quickly learned, the number of volunteer hours members were required to work was daunting to begin with, and once additional hours were added on for punishment, it began to feel like an impossible task. And it didn't help that so many hours that could have been spent doing the volunteer work were spent at meetings for the CLL to *discuss* doing the volunteer work and giving status reports on our various jobs.

I missed the job sign-up meeting because I had some trivial little obligation. It was my son's fifth-grade graduation, that's all. In my absence, one of the other moms signed me up for the job of "Brunch Chair." This had *nothing* to do with her innate sense that I would be great at *throwing* a brunch, and *everything* to do with the fact that she'd been to my house and thought it would be a great place to *have a brunch*. It sounded like an easy job, though. After all, I'd had people over for brunch before. How hard could it be?

Very hard, apparently. This was not some casual little brunch. It was a huge formal affair, which I soon found out I could not have catered (even at my own expense). My usual fallback of buying ready-made quiches at Costco was a big no-no as well. Everything had to be handmade expressly for the brunch following only the approved CLL recipes as outlined in the brunch binder. Oh yes, this brunch came with its own binder! I found this out when it mysteriously appeared on my doorstep one morning. It was shiny, white, and three inches thick. All three inches were filled with neatly outlined instructions on how to put on this annual brunch. There were details on foods, beverages, invitations, and flower arrangements (which also had to be made by hand), including colored photographs of each item, and then some, from the ten previous brunches. There were diagrams of table arrangements and settings and information regarding how to "sign out" the CLL china and linens from whomever had the job of maintaining that. Yes, maintaining the CLL's tableware was another job one could sign up for, or be signed up for in one's absence.

You might think I was going to be throwing a brunch for the Queen of England. But no, it was a brunch for the princesses of the CLL. They wanted me to do all of that work, spend countless hours toiling away in the kitchen cooking, arranging flowers, and folding napkins into swans for the very girls who were supposed to be volunteering for the needy. Seemed to me like it would have made a lot more sense to have a brunch to feed the needy themselves. Cut out the middleman. At the very least I thought we could forgo the brunch and just donate the money it would have cost to put it on to the needy. I thought wrong. This was the way the CLL had always done it and will always do it. Instead of serving the needy, I would be serving the privileged. Moreover, I'd be doing it in pantyhose.

This just did not sit well with me. And the more I thought about it, the more I came to dread it. I had a heart-to-heart with my daughter, and she had actually come to the same conclusion. She had been given a job as well—Cultural Committee Co-Chair. And if you think that meant she was going to plan some sort of cultural event for the needy, or benefiting the needy, you'd be wrong. Being cultured was right up there with wearing pantyhose on the list of what was required of the members of the CLL. We were done.

Quitting was only slightly more difficult than joining. I had to submit my written intention to do so in triplicate to several different muckety mucks and then await their decision. I would of course forfeit any dues I'd already paid (I figured as much; they had to pay for that brunch somehow, right?) and sign a document stating that I was resigning with the full understanding that I would be doing so in "bad standing" and therefore would never, under any circumstances, be allowed to rejoin the CLL. Fine by me.

. . . .

I had set out to do some good in the world, side by side with my daughter. Would we still volunteer together if nobody was forcing us? Could we find something useful to do even if we weren't wearing pantyhose? Was it possible that the CLL cornered the market on volunteerism? I kind of doubted it since somebody somewhere out there had to be doing good deeds while the ladies were brunching and attending meetings. I had already found some of those people when I became involved with ACT Today! and ran Wyatt's Run. I was planning to stay involved with that organization, but thought it would be nice to find some other volunteer opportunities that my kids and I could do together whenever our schedules permitted. Since we wouldn't have to wear hose, the boys could join in, too.

And so, I put "do a charity project with the kids" on that list of mine and set out to find some volunteer opportunities. "How about 'Heal the Bay'?" one of my sons asked. He had heard about it at school where the students are required to complete a certain number of community service hours every year. Heal the Bay was one of the ones on a list the school had provided, a list that I'd tucked in the file labeled "school" without reading it. I dug it out and found that in addition to Heal the Bay there were a number of other organizations that needed help and welcomed kid volunteers. Heal the Bay is an organization that helps clean up beaches and educate people about the consequences of pollution. Remember that movie *Happy Feet?* Remember the penguin with the plastic rings that hold six packs of soda (also known as polymer rings) around his neck? Well, that really can happen, along with a laundry list of other terrible things. The boys and I showed up at one of their clean up the beach events early one morning, and for a couple of hours we worked alongside other volunteers picking up trash at Will Rogers State Beach. I was shocked at how much Styrofoam there was scattered around in the sand. Those cheap coolers that you can pick up at grocery stores break apart really easily and the result is tiny pieces of Styrofoam that look a lot like food to fish and other marine animals. They ingest that, and then we ingest them. Gross. We logged our findings on a form that Heal the Bay provided and after our shift, we combined our collected trash with that of the other volunteers to make a very sizable mound of crap that shouldn't have been on the beach.

It was easy work and it was nice to be out there together. Several people who were there just to enjoy the beach came up and thanked us for what we were doing. It felt very good to have made a difference and to be recognized for that. I could see that my boys were proud of themselves, and I was very proud of them, so proud that I took them to Bubba Gump's Shrimp restaurant on the Santa Monica Pier afterward to celebrate our accomplishment.

The next time we volunteered together my daughter came, too. We went to the My Stuff Bags warehouse in Westlake Village, CA. My Stuff Bags is an organization that puts together duffle bags filled with comfort items and basic necessities that are then distributed to kids who have been taken out of unsafe domestic situations by child protective services. Often these kids are removed with little or no notice and don't have time to gather any of their belongings, which only makes them feel even more afraid. It helps them to have something that's their very own, to know that someone cares for them enough to provide items that are nice and new. I know it may sound like a small gesture in light of the emotional turmoil they are feeling, but it's something—and sometimes it's more than they've had in a long time.

The kids and I were put to work assembly-line style. First we got bags ready to be packaged, attaching blank luggage tags where the recipient's name would later be added. Then we filled the bags with toiletries, blankets, stuffed animals, coloring books, etc.

As part of the process, we learned how to make the blankets from inexpensive fleece. It seems that they are always running out of blankets. We measured and cut the fabric according to the specifications, cut strips and tied knots to make fringe. This was not rocket science. We managed to make quite a few while we were there. It felt great to do something to help comfort these kids.

My daughter had the wonderful idea of starting a club at school in which students could make blankets together. She asked the woman at the front desk about where to buy the fleece (they get a great discount from a store downtown) and if she could have a copy of the instructions and specs for making the different sizes. Kayla had really gotten into the spirit of what we were doing and wanted to lead others in helping out this great organization. Again, I felt nothin' but pride.

The boys also completely "got it"—they understood exactly the impact that their efforts would have on kids in crisis. They asked me at lunch afterward (somehow our volunteer efforts always led to meals out) if we could go back there again soon. I pointed out that they had by then completed their community service requirements for the school year. "That's OK," they replied. "We want to do it. It was fun." Well all right! I'm going to pat myself on the back here. It was much more fun to do charity work together as a family than I'd thought it would be. And without the confines of an organization like the CLL, we could do it at our own convenience and without it feeling like it was a punishment. I'd worried that if there was no external structure we wouldn't manage to get out there and volunteer, but that wasn't the case. I just needed to make the effort and set aside the time. It was a wonderful learning and bonding experience and that was all the motivation I needed to keep on doing it.

I crossed "do a charity project with the kids" off my list but added it to my family's life. Not only are we finding ways to make a difference together, the kids are finding ways to volunteer on their own and encouraging their friends to get involved, too. When you're making your own list, think about including something that will benefit others. Believe me, it will benefit you just as much, if not more so. And, if you have kids, let them in on it. What an amazing gift to give your children: a way to find a sense of purpose and a source of pride. It can be as simple as giving away old toys, clothes, and books, or if you have some time, research some local charities that permit kids to volunteer. Whether you get involved on an ongoing basis or just once in a while, whether you stick to one particular cause or spread your efforts among multiple organizations is really up to you. To do good is to feel good. No pantyhose required.

#6 Do a charity project with the kids

THREE

LET'S GET PHYSICAL

This chapter has nothing to do with Olivia Newton John, slicked up body builders, terry cloth headbands, or leg warmers. Well, maybe it's just a little bit about leg warmers, but mostly it's about three different physical goals I put on my list. And mind you, as I set out to "take an adult ballet class," "fly on the trapeze," and "try yoga at the beach," I expected these activities to be a challenge to my body only; I gave no thought to my emotions. But just like those high-cut spandex leotards from the eighties, I couldn't have been more wrong.

. . . .

When I was growing up I took a lot of ballet classes. So many, in fact, that you'd think I'd have gotten pretty good at it, but you'd be wrong. While it seemed I was built for ballet—I had naturally turned out feet with high arches, strong legs, and a fairly high tolerance for pain—I was lacking in confidence. I focused on the things I couldn't do rather than the many, many, things I *could* do.

It hadn't always been this way. In fact, I was pretty self-assured when I first started taking lessons. My mother had signed me up for a beginning ballet class at Chatham College's summer camp for the arts. In a sea of other eight-year-olds, I stood out, and at the end of the camp session, the teacher suggested that I audition for the Pittsburgh Ballet Theatre School (PBT School). I auditioned, and I must have done pretty well, because they accepted me and promptly placed me in a class with mostly older girls who had several years of ballet training under their tutus.

Every class began with barre exercises, which I was decent at and could handle. If I forgot the instructions the teacher gave, I copied what the girl in front of me did, and with the barre to hold on to, balance wasn't an issue. But when it came to floor work, I had no such crutch. The teacher would call out moves like *entrechat*, *jeté*, *glassad*, and *pas de chat*, and I would rack my brain trying to figure out what she was talking about. My own French was limited to *Merde!*, which is what I uttered under my breath every time my teacher lined us up for *chaînés* turns, or any other kind of turns for that matter. You see, like Zoolander, I could not turn to my left. This is not to say that I turned well to my right, because I didn't. In fact, there were quite a few things that no matter how hard I tried, I just couldn't master. The other girls would turn, and I would fall off center. They would do a slow *passe* to *arabesque* and *ponche* during an adagio, and I couldn't balance on one leg.

I was so worried I'd make a fool of myself that whenever the teacher called us to the floor, I'd suddenly have to pee. Or I'd remember I had to leave early. Or I'd clumsily turn, completely off center in dizzying fashion only to then excuse myself with claims of a muscle cramp or some other trumped-up injury. If only I could take my younger self aside. I would talk to her about not giving up, learning how to admit it when help is needed, knowing that there is honor in perseverance, and that sometimes hard work more than makes up for lack of talent.

I never wanted a career in dance, but I still longed to be able to do what the other girls could do with proficiency. And so I took lessons at PBT School—but only sporadically. I'd go for a while, get frustrated, and quit, only to return again after a year or two. I dabbled on and off this way until tenth grade, when I quit PBT School for the last time. I fit in a few classes in college. And then, one day, I just stopped. If it had been due to a lack of interest, then I wouldn't have looked back. But it wasn't a lack of interest, it was a lack of confidence and ability combined with an extremely debilitating case of self-criticism. As much as I loved ballet, I was willing to take it away from myself rather than risk being laughed at. And so, when I made that list of all the things I thought I would've done by now, I included "take an adult ballet class." I was determined to put on those tights once more and see what I could do about my limitations in dance. At the time, I thought my physical limitations were the only ones I'd be revisiting.

I signed up for a *gentle* ballet class for adults at the California Dance Theatre. This was a class designed specifically for people who hadn't danced in years or who were returning to dance after an injury. My classmates had no intention of becoming prima ballerinas and there were no expectations of greatness. These were women who danced simply because they loved to dance. When I arrived at the class, I sized up the other women. I wasn't going to be the best, but I probably wasn't going to be the worst, either. I went there hoping to get through a class with confidence, fully commit to the floor work, and not let anything keep me from at least trying my best.

I was hopeful that things would be different, but in the end things were just about the same as they had been twenty years ago. I did fine at the barre, and then, as soon as the teacher had us go out onto the floor I started to panic. I thought I was somewhere in the middle of the pack skill-wise, but when it came to the floor work I realized that I was actually toward the bottom. I wasn't able to execute the moves and quickly became self-conscious. I drifted to the corner, opting to watch instead of participate.

As in the past, I was pretty upset with myself. This time, however, it was for different reasons. It wasn't my inability to do the moves that I was beating myself up over, it was the quitting. As I watched the other dancers move across the floor, I wondered to myself why I couldn't do what they were doing. Then it struck me. How could I know how to do something that I hadn't ever learned how to do? It wasn't lack of ability that was holding me back. I was no less equipped than these other women. Heck, if anything I was more so. What they had that I didn't, was know-how. I'd never been taught the step-by-step mechanics of ballet. I hadn't stayed in beginning ballet for more than just those few lessons at camp before I started the intermediate class at the PBT School, so I'd missed out on learning a lot of the basics. But I was determined not to let it happen again.

After class I approached the teacher and asked her something I'd never thought to ask any ballet teacher in the past. "Will you please help me learn how to do those steps?" And she did. She stayed after class and gave me a half-hour private lesson during which she broke the moves down for me, offering me instruction, correction, and encouragement. That's not to say that I left that day ready for a solo in Swan Lake. But I did leave there with hope that one day I would be better. Understanding what my body was supposed to be doing, and getting it to do those things, was going to take practice. It was going to take commitment from me not to get frustrated and quit, to allow myself the time it takes to really learn how to do something. It would involve both my body and my mind. Once I saw the connection between the two a lightbulb went on. I realized this was going to be challenging *and* fun. And so, even though I officially crossed "take an adult ballet class" off of my list, I still take a class now and then. When I do I'm not the best, but I'm okay with that, because I am the best that I can be. And that is always good enough.

#7 ~~Take an adult ballet class~~

. . . .

In taking on my ballet challenge I'd put my current self back into a situation where my younger self had left off. It gave me the opportunity to take a closer look at some unresolved childhood emotional issues from a more mature and wiser perspective. I experienced something similar when I took on another of my physical challenges, "fly on the trapeze."

I can trace my fascination with the trapeze back to a very early memory: when I was five, my Grandma Joan took me to see the Ringling Brothers and Barnum & Bailey Circus. Here's what I remember from that day: I ate roasted peanuts from a red and white paper bag; I saw elephants wearing little fez hats and felt sorry for them; I saw clowns for the first time and immediately decided I hated them; and I saw a woman fly.

On a platform high above the ground stood a woman who was long, lean, and impossibly elegant. She was poised there above the crowd, dressed in a dazzling sequined leotard. It seemed as if stars shot from her body as that costume caught the spotlight. When she took hold of the trapeze bar the whole audience appeared to draw in its breath with anticipation. Suddenly, she leapt into the air and flew silently across the tent.

She was completely fearless as she did trick after trick, flipping around on the bar like it took no effort at all. I was mesmerized by her. I wanted to *be* her. Then, there was a man swinging toward her. He was upside-down hanging by his knees, his muscle-bound arms outstretched and ready to catch her. I remember thinking it was as if a fairy tale was being played out in the air. The woman a sparkly princess, the strong man her prince.

I was so taken by the aerial act that I had actually stood up and wandered closer to get a better view. I didn't even realize I had done it until a security guard tapped me on the shoulder and asked me if I was lost. He helped me back to my seat. I was still in such awe from what I'd seen that I didn't even mind getting lectured by my grandmother.

The following Christmas I was given Dr. Seuss's *My Book About Me* as a gift from my parents. It was a fill-in-the-blank book with questions for me to answer, such as how many windows and doors there were in my house, how long my longest swim had been, and how many freckles I had. At the end of the book was a double page with one last fill-in-the-blank sentence. "When I grow up I want to be _____." The pages were filled with career options: nurse, teacher, blacksmith, cartoonist, soldier, banker, etc. My sister, who had been "helping" me fill in my book, wrote "nurse" in thick red marker. I immediately took a pencil, crossed "nurse" out, and wrote, "trapez lady." I wasn't sure about the spelling, but I knew that was what I wanted to be when I grew up.

I remember the little girl who wrote that; she truly believed she could do anything. She was very much on my mind when I was making my list. I wondered what she would have thought about the woman she'd become, the one who hadn't gone after any of the things she'd claimed she wanted to do in life. I wanted to make that little girl proud. I wanted to do something for her so she would know I loved her and that I had not forgotten her. It felt very much like I was making a formal promise to her when I wrote "fly on the trapeze" on my list. There it was in black and white, just like in *My Book About Me*. But this time, I was going to make sure I did it.

By the time I called the New York Trapeze School's Santa Monica location I had already completed almost all of my other challenges. I really wanted to do this for my little-girl self, but my grown-up self was more than a little bit scared. I wasn't completely sure what would happen when I got to the top of that platform and the moment of truth came. Would I chicken out? Would I jump? There was only one way to find out. I dialed their number and the man on the other end of the phone told me they offered classes every day, and I was in luck, because there was space the following morning in the 10:45 a.m. class. Before I could talk myself out of it I told the man I'd be there. No turning back.

The next day I drove along Pacific Coast Highway to Santa Monica. It's a beautiful drive, and it was a gorgeous day. I was really nervous, but also very excited. I'm sure I was shaking as I climbed the ladder for my first attempt to fly on the trapeze. That platform seemed so much higher than when I was looking up from the ground. I stood as the instructors had told me, toes over the edge of the platform. I had to lean out in order to grab the bar with both hands. That alone nearly scared me enough to back out, but I was determined to give this a try. There was a sturdy net below me, and I was harnessed tightly. It didn't make me feel any safer, though. All I could think about was how high off the ground I was, and how fast I was going to be moving. I was worried about following the instructions they had given me.

What if I didn't remember what to do? What if I couldn't hold on? Before I could change my mind and climb down the instructor ordered, "Ready!" This was my cue to bend my knees. "Hep!" That was the command for go, and in this case, go meant jump. Jump off the platform. As scared as I was, and as against every instinct I had, I jumped. I was moving so fast that my stomach kind of lurched as if I were on a roller coaster. I gripped that bar as tightly as I could and swung out toward the ocean. As soon as I was swinging the other way the instructor shouted at me to put my feet up and over the bar. I did not hesitate. I honestly felt that if I did not follow his directions to the letter, I would fall off and die, net or no net.

Then he yelled, "Let go!" I let go and was swinging the other way again. This time, I was hanging by my knees, back arched, arms reaching out. I was once again swinging toward the ocean. It was all happening so fast. It seemed I had just gotten into that position when I felt the momentum shift. I was swinging the other direction again, and the instructor ordered me to grab the bar with my hands and pull my feet back through. I felt another shift in momentum, and I was swinging out toward the ocean once more, with my hands clutching the bar above me and my feet pointed down toward the net below. "Now, let go!" The instructor shouted. I did and found myself falling into the net. The ride was over. My heart was beating so fast that there was no question I was still alive.

"Excellent," the instructor praised me. "Next time, when I say to let go, I will tell you to kick your legs forward, back, forward and then I want you to bring your knees quickly into your chest and tuck your chin. You're going to do a backflip." Was he high, I wondered? Oh, but he wasn't. The next attempt went more smoothly than the first. I was less scared this time because I knew what to expect. I did not, however, do the back flip as instructed. I just landed as I had before, on my butt. On my third try I did it! I managed to get through the entire process and finished with a perfect back flip dismount. And I did it several more times, each time feeling a little more confident and a little less petrified.

I had done my backflip, but the class wasn't over yet. We were moving on to "catching," which meant I would be caught by one of the male instructors who would be hanging by his knees on another bar. I was scared all over again. There would come a moment when

I would have to allow this guy to basically pull me off of my trapeze. Aside from the harness, he'd be the only thing holding me up there, whereas before I was responsible for myself. I would have to trust him, which for a control freak like me, was no easy task.

I climbed the ladder once again, took hold of the bar, and waited for the "ready, hep" commands. There was no time to think. I was swinging out, I was swinging back, feet up and over the bar, I let go and reached out, and lo and behold, there he was, my very own prince, just like the one I'd seen at the circus all those years ago. His were arms outstretched, his face suddenly inches from mine. "C'mon girl! Let's go!" he said calmly with a bright smile, and he grabbed my wrists. There we were, the two of us, swinging double, he hanging upside down on his bar by his knees, and me below him, arms up, hands around his wrists as he held onto mine. I was facing the ocean again and then, just as suddenly as the trick started, it was finished. "Toes up!" my prince commanded and he let go. I plopped down into the net on my bottom, in a seated position.

"And how many years of gymnastics have you had?" one of the other instructors asked.

"None!" I answered. I was quite pleased with myself that she thought I'd had gymnastics training. I took it to mean that I'd done something right, and that I looked good up there. Maybe five-year-old me was on to something. Maybe I could have been a trapeze lady after all. I pictured my younger self in my mind, smiling ear-to-ear, proud of what I'd just accomplished. This was as close to a full-circle moment as I'd ever come. I'd fulfilled a very big promise to myself, and that's the most satisfying kind to keep.

Oh how I wish the story ended here. The wonderful feeling of flying on that trapeze, the view of the Pacific Ocean and the amusement park rides below me, and my Oprah-esque full-circle moment. That is the stuff of dreams and fairy tales, though. We live in reality, where things can and do go very wrong. At the very end of my two-hour lesson the teacher said we could each go up and take one last turn. I was feeling really euphoric just then. I was physically exhausted, yes, but I was also high on adrenaline. I had a moment where an inner voice told me to stay on the ground, not to tempt fate, that this had been an amazing experience and I should end it on a high note. But I got cocky.

Who the hell was that voice to tell me I shouldn't continue doing something I'd waited my whole life to try? Why shouldn't I savor every last second of that experience? Was that voice the one that always kept me from putting myself out there, the one that told me I wasn't strong enough, or good enough, or worthy enough to achieve my goals? It didn't sound like that old voice; it sounded quite calm and kind, actually. Rational. The voice made sense. I decided not to listen anyway.

Before I ascended for my last turn of the day I took a giant stand against that rational voice by asking if I might be able to do a different trick than the one I'd learned. The one I'd been doing over and over again for two hours had gone swimmingly, so I thought perhaps I should try something that one of the regular students was working on. Muscles fatigued, I climbed that ladder one last time and attempted to do—wait for it—the upside down splits trick!

Only I never made it upside down and I never did the splits. What happened was that I switched to autopilot, and I started doing the same trick I'd been doing. Instead of putting one foot on the bar, knee bent and my other leg straight up, thigh pressed against the bar, I started to put both feet over the bar. I realized my mistake and tried to adjust my body into the proper position. In doing so, my left foot slipped and my right leg came away from the bar. The one thing I remember the teacher telling me was to be absolutely sure to keep that right thigh pressed against the bar no matter what. But there it was, away from the bar and dropping quickly. It felt like I had a very bad Charlie horse in my left hamstring, and then I felt a very distinct pop. It was my tendon coming off of my pelvic bone, although I didn't know it at the time. What I did know was something was definitely wrong and I was still swinging. I let go, landed safely in the net, and managed to get to the edge where a couple of the teachers helped me get down onto the ground. I hobbled to my car and drove home, deflated.

It was clearly my own fault that this had happened, and I was very embarrassed. I had no business trying a new trick in the very last few minutes of my very first class. That voice, it turns out, was not the old mean one bent on derailing me, it was the voice of reason—my instinct, if you will—trying in vain to keep me safe.

After a day or two of icing my leg and trying to stay off of it, I reluctantly went to see an orthopedist. According to him, and my MRI results, my hamstring was torn and the tendon was completely off the bone. Fixing this required surgery, titanium anchors, and four weeks on crutches followed by six weeks of physical therapy. This was not what I'd hoped to get out of my trapeze adventure.

Getting injured did not negate all of the fun, positive, promise-fulfilling aspects of the experience, but it did make me pause to think. In the end, I decided not to let it spoil the wonder of the trapeze challenge. After all, I had that amazing full-circle moment, even if the circle did turn into a bubble that was suddenly popped by my razor-sharp stupidity.

I'd gone into this experience with my eyes wide open, knowing that it would be challenging physically, and it turned out I was right on the money with that one. What I didn't anticipate, as had proved to be the case with many of my adventures, was how many life lessons I was going learn. Here's what I got out of this one: I have excellent instincts and ought to listen to them, especially when NOT listening to them could result in injury. It's okay to say I'm finished when I've gotten what I wanted out of something. There isn't always a prize at the bottom of that cereal box; sometimes there's a scalpel, stitches, crutches, and a physical therapist (or worse). I should always take responsibility and act accordingly. After all, I am the one who did this to myself, nobody else. Because I can admit that, I know I will be smarter next time. Oh yes, I've prepaid for another lesson. I'll bet a sparkly leotard that one day soon I will pull off that upside-down splits trick, safely and without incident.

#8 ~~Fly on the trapeze~~

. . . .

Flying on the trapeze was one of the challenges that pushed me outside my comfort zone (way, way, way outside my comfort zone). I think it would seem pretty exotic to the vast majority of people. Not so with another physical challenge from my list, yoga. Here in California, yoga is a mainstream form of exercise—there's a yoga class around every corner. Despite its availability, however, I had never tried it. I am a creature of habit, never quick to shift gears or stray from the beaten path—especially if I'm the one who beat the path in the first place. Yes, "If it ain't broke, don't fix it" has been my philosophy for just about everything, including my thrice-weekly workouts.

I don't know if it's fear of the unknown or fear of falling on my face in front of other people, but it's definitely fear that lies at the root of my reluctance to try new things. This applied to everything from laundry detergent (Tide) to underwear (Commando Girl Shorts), and exercise was no exception. When I drew up my list, I'd been going to the same kickboxing class for seven years. I loved it, but it was high time I mixed it up a little. Even the other "regulars" in my trusty kickboxing class did other types of exercise now and then. For instance, quite a few of them practiced yoga. Yoga sounded like the perfect yin to kickboxing's yang—I thought a healthy dose of peace and tranquillity could be the perfect balance for all that adrenaline-pumping punching and kicking. Plus, they had really cute yoga pants at Lulu Lemon, and I'd never had a reason to buy some before.

So buy some I did, and I put "try yoga" on my list. Not just "try yoga," but "try yoga at the beach" (everything is better at the beach). I live in Los Angeles; there are several beaches within driving distance of my house. I rarely go, however, and so I left that goal undone for quite some time, always figuring that I would get to it one day. In the meantime, it was business as usual—kickboxing: Monday, Wednesday, Friday.

Then one Tuesday morning (my kickboxing teacher's day off), I decided to take a little jog in my neighborhood. After my botched 5k mission, sticking close to home seemed like my best bet. That particular day my route took me down the main road of my development right past the community center. I looked over as I jogged past, and guess what? There was a yoga class about to begin. I started thinking that maybe this was fate, and maybe the beach wasn't essential to the whole yoga experience after all. Besides, I saw someone I'd been meaning to call—my friend Joe.

I'd originally met Joe and his wife Erica through our kids, who were classmates. Erica and I had become very good friends; we talked for hours about teachers, sports, problems at school, causes, parenting, goals, dreams, etc. We quickly developed a mutual admiration society and recognized in each other a similar parenting style and value system. Rarely did I make any difficult decision involving the kids that I didn't discuss with Erica first, and she always had a wise and sympathetic response. She worked as a professional mediator, so you can imagine how levelheaded she was.

It hadn't been long since, at the age of forty-three, Erica had died while snowboarding with her family in Mammoth, CA. They had a house up there and went practically every weekend. The kids snowboarded on a national level, and she and her husband were both experts as well. It's difficult to accept that she is gone and that she died suddenly doing something she was so good at.

About two weeks before her death, Erica and I had talked for a couple hours and she'd told me about her upcoming trip to Cuba, which was the realization of a lifelong dream. She was going with her parents as part of a volunteer group, taking medicine to AIDS patients there. That was Erica for you; she was always volunteering and doing good works. And she also was always busy living. Not just planning to live, but really actually doing it. She'd traveled a lot, experienced a lot of things, and helped a lot of people, including me.

Now I was standing there with her husband, Joe. I hadn't seen him since the Shiva. That's a Jewish tradition—a darn good one if you ask me—that involves friends and family gathering together when someone has died to share prayer, thoughts, stories, and, of course, food. Everyone is there for the purpose of processing someone's death, and it's easy to talk about the person and give words of comfort. But what about after the dust has settled? What about when you bump into someone at yoga who's suffered a loss like this? What do you say then?

Well, I didn't say anything before the teacher arrived and offered to lend me her mat and although my darling Lulu Lemon yoga pants were back at home with the tags still attached, I decided I would stay. I got a spot at the front of the room, right by the teacher. That way she could marvel at what a natural I was. I soon found out that there was nothing natural about yoga for me. The stuff about flow and breathing and working with your body and not forcing movement or pushing past where your body wanted to be at that moment was the opposite of everything I'd ever learned in ballet and kickboxing.

I'd always been taught if you weren't in pain you weren't working hard enough, and I approached yoga with that mentality. At one point the instructor had us lying down on our backs, hands reaching up to pull our legs in toward our chests. I was concentrating hard on forcing my leg to go beyond where it really should have gone in hopes that the instructor would notice my great flexibility. If she did, she didn't mention it. What she did mention was that I was not breathing. As it turns out, breathing is a big thing in yoga.

It wasn't until she pointed it out to me that I realized she was right. I wasn't breathing. I was holding my breath and trying to force myself into something that was beyond my ability, beyond my anatomy. The whole idea that I could work within my comfort zone in order to eventually expand that comfort zone was new to me, but very, very interesting. Once I focused on getting the positions right without pulling something in the process, I started to really feel it.

On my walk home I thought about what I'd learned from my "try yoga at the beach rec center" experience. Yoga did prove to be the yin to kickboxing's yang, but it also proved to be a great full-body workout. By the end of the class I felt less like I'd had a kick-ass workout and more like I'd had a deep-tissue massage. That's a feeling I could get used to.

I am so glad I let go of the "at the beach" part of my "try yoga at the beach" challenge. I had broken free of my physical routine by trying a different form of exercise. I had also broken free of my mental routine by allowing myself to modify the challenge. In doing so I discovered something really essential to the concept of the list; it should be liberating, not restricting. If, when you start tackling your own list, you find that there is some aspect of a goal that's holding you back from an opportunity to achieve it, you can change it. It is *your* list. It's about you, for you, and written by you. If I'd fulfilled my yoga challenge at the beach instead of at the community center, it would have taken me a lot longer. More important, I wouldn't have had a chance to talk with my friend Joe after class.

I asked him how he was doing. "I'm good, life is good," he said. He shared with me that he'd been to counseling, had read Eckhart Tolle's book *A New Earth* (which I have also read, but am thinking I need to reread), and that he had come to a place where he was at peace. He missed Erica's physical presence, of course, but the love they shared hadn't gone anywhere. He kept it safe in his heart were he could be at home with it every day. That blew me away. I was so happy that he was happy. I know Erica would be, too.

#9 ~~Try yoga at the rec center (the challenge formerly known as "Try yoga at the beach")~~

. . . .

I now know that my physical challenges weren't just physical. While I thoroughly enjoyed that aspect of the challenges (aside from getting injured), it was the emotional aspects that had the lasting benefit. When you are making your list, I hope you will include a few physical challenges of your own. They don't have to be death defying. In fact, I highly discourage that. I do, however, suggest you to throw your body a curve ball by doing something new and different or taking another stab at something that you used to do but quit. You will find that exercising the body exercises the mind, and vice versa. In the end, you will be stronger in both.

ARE YOU THERE, GOD?
IT'S ME, SUSAN.

One would think that by the time a person reaches middle age they would know what religion they are. I did not know, which would have been fine except for the fact that I really *wanted* to know. I wanted to belong somewhere, to feel that I was a part of *some* congregation. So I put "Go church shopping" on my list.

. . . .

Religiously speaking, I am a mutt. My father was raised Methodist, but now says he's an Atheist. My mother is a follower of "Science of Mind" but was raised Jewish, although she never had a bat mitzvah. Apparently she was kicked out of Hebrew school for telling dirty jokes. Once they were married and had us kids, the question of what religion we should be became unavoidable. They finally agreed on Unitarian Universalist. If you aren't familiar with this religion, it falls under the Protestant umbrella and prides itself on what I like to describe as an "I'm Okay, You're Okay" attitude.

Basically this means that you can believe what you want and not be judged for it. Not too shabby, if you ask me. The thing is that my grandparents didn't seem to think it was any kind of religion at all. At least not one they wanted their grandchildren raised in. I remember on many occasions Grandma Joan (my maternal grandmother) saying, "You are Jewish, honey. I don't care where you go on Sundays. You're Jewish. Your mother is Jewish, you are Jewish." This was usually followed by a lengthy lecture about how if I lived in Poland during World War II (God forbid!) that I certainly would be Jewish enough for Hitler.

Grandma Campbell (my father's mother) was more subtle. That's Methodist for passive aggressive. If we were visiting her and our parents weren't around, she would take us down to the Methodist church and walk us around to meet all of the church ladies. "What a pretty little girl," they'd remark patting my head.

"Yes, yes, such a pretty little thing," my grandmother would reply. "She doesn't attend a Methodist church you know, but Jesus loves her anyway."

At Grandma Joan's we'd have kugel and matzo ball soup, gefilte fish, and brisket. She tried relentlessly to make me eat chopped liver, but I never could bring myself to swallow it. For dessert my grandmother always had something exotic. Never one to shy away from the spotlight she'd say, "It's my pineapple upside-down cake, Suzala, now how do you love that?" She often asked this question about anything from desserts to her new carpeting, although it really wasn't much of a question since the answer was contained within it.

"I love it?" I'd answer.

"Well of course you do," she'd beam, "*Everybody* loves my _____ (fill in the blank here)!"

At Grandma Campbell's we'd have ham, peas, mashed white potatoes, and white bread with butter and a big glass of milk. There was always dessert. "Just a little something," she'd say as she emerged from the kitchen with some gorgeous array of hand-decorated sugar cookies, too pretty to eat. "Just a little something," is Methodist for, "I spent all day making these so you'd better oooh and ahhh over them for at least ten minutes." Like I said. Subtle.

We learned the different ways of the different sides of our family and were able to fit in enough to blend, but not enough to really belong. There's a big difference there, especially for a child. And while we were "okay" at the Unitarian church, I never really felt like it was a spiritual home.

Flash-forward a couple of decades and I faced the same dilemma my parents had. I married an Episcopalian, which is kind of like "Catholic Lite." They have a lot of the same traditions; the Episcopalians just seem to take them a wee bit less seriously. Oh, and the priests are allowed to have sex and get married (but probably not in that order). My husband was brought up by two parents who were both Episcopalian, and to really cement the deal, his godfather was an Episcopal priest.

I was sort of a mixed bag in terms of my heritage, but all the while I was learning to accept myself, it never occurred to me that anyone else might have an issue with accepting me. The neighborhood where I grew up was predominantly Jewish, and at school there was a fairly even mix of Jewish kids and Christian kids from almost every form of Christianity from Greek Orthodox, to Catholic, to Baptist, to Presbyterian, and then some. Nobody ever raised an eyebrow at anyone's beliefs or lack of beliefs. It didn't occur to me that there was anything about me, at least not religiously, that could be of concern to anyone else.

That is until I was about to marry into the family of an Episcopalian. My husband's mother, bless her heart, actually sat me down to tell me that she loved me very much—one of her best friends was

Jewish—and that she had made a special trip down south to break the news to the family that Kevin would be marrying a Jew (but a very nice one).

I didn't know whether to say, "Thank you," or, "Screw you." But in an effort to keep peace I said nothing at all. And I have continued to bite my tongue when necessary. Funny how quick they were to label me when I had always struggled to figure out what I was myself. Why was it that I was "Jewish" and not "Methodist" or "Unitarian?" Wasn't I just as much one thing as another—and just as little one thing as another? I guess my grandmother was right. If I was Jewish enough for Hitler, I was Jewish.

My husband attended church only when his parents were in town (sorry, Kevin, the jig is finally up). Since he wasn't a regular anywhere, he and I agreed to look at several different churches. We hadn't felt any pressure to go before we had children, but once we did, it seemed like the responsible thing to do. A child should have a religious and spiritual education, shouldn't they? Or should they? Are the two one and the same?

We began attending the First Presbyterian Church of Hollywood, which seemed to be a good fit for us. It was full of very welcoming people from all walks of life. The movie stars and the homeless all sat together in worship, and that gave me the feeling that if I couldn't belong there, I couldn't belong anywhere. We became members. In a prime example of the blind leading the blind, I even taught a summer Sunday school class, and surprise, surprise, I actually enjoyed it. I felt like what I was teaching the kids was the truth. Our God was a loving one, an accepting one, and we were not to judge each other, but to leave that to Him.

Unfortunately, several years after we became members of that church it came out publicly against ordaining homosexual clergy. This bothered me for many reasons. First of all, I had joined the congregation under the premise that this was a place where everyone was equal in the eyes of God. We were not to judge others, yet here were the higher-ups at the church, saying for all intents and purposes that people who happened to be born homosexual were not capable of leading the flock. Really? What was it exactly that they had done that was so bad? I mean convicted felons could get ordained via the Internet, people who had been found guilty of robbery, rape, or murder. But if you happened to be gay, no way! It just didn't make sense to me. How could a church claim to be so loving, and accepting, and open to everyone, and then come out strongly against one group of people who have done absolutely nothing to warrant that type of discrimination?

That was the end of our attendance of the First Presbyterian Church of Hollywood. The place where I had finally felt I belonged turned out to be someplace I didn't want to belong. Years went by and we didn't go to church of any kind—happy years, actually. Once in a while, when the kids would be asked what religion they were, I had a flash of guilt. Had I passed on to them the same sense of not truly belonging anywhere? I decided to include church shopping on my list. I would employ what I have come to call the Goldilocks approach. I was going to try on different religions until I found one that fit just right.

It wasn't long before the first opportunity arose, in the form of an invitation to one of our neighbor's bat mitzvahs. My husband balked at the idea of having to sit through the service—he'd heard from our kids how long and boring these things were— but I was determined to be thorough in my research and so we went. My husband even wore a yamaka (covered his bald spot nicely, if you ask me). The bat mitzvah was in a conservative temple; that alone probably tripled the length of the service. I was half dozing when I heard the rabbi say something about what it means to be Jewish. My ears perked up— that was what I'd been waiting for. But pretty much all that he mentioned could be (and is) also applied to any religion.

The rabbi talked and talked, the cantor sang and sang, I waited and waited for some lightbulb to go off, some bell to ring signaling to me that I was home. But it didn't happen. After three-plus hours, I wasn't any closer to knowing what I was—aside from very hungry. At the Kiddish luncheon there was more praying before we could eat.

The party later that night was lavish and extravagant. The girl of honor was all decked out in her party dress and made a huge entrance singing a Britney Spears song, of all things! There were toasts by family members and then a lengthy video of a show celebrating the Bat Mitzvah girl's life, acted out by every immediate and extended family member.

This was some party. The bat mitzvah to end all bat mitzvahs if you will. Held at the Skirball Cultural Center, there was a cocktail reception with passed hors d'oeuvres and an open bar, followed by the main event, which included several buffets featuring gourmet foods from around the world, flower arrangements the likes of which I'd never seen, a DJ, and dancers. I had an amazing time eating, drinking, dancing, talking with friends and neighbors, and celebrating this girl's rite of passage. I didn't feel any more Jewish than I had the day before, but I did feel relieved that I didn't have to throw this type of party three times over (so far none of the kids has asked to have a bar or bat mitzvah of their own). It surely cost about ten times what my wedding did, and so for very different reasons than in World War II days, I could not afford to be Jewish—at least not until my kids were over the age of thirteen.

Our foray into Judaism continued when our dear friends, a gay couple, invited us (the Cross's) to a Shabbat dinner, at which they served vegan Chinese food. It sounds like a comedian's bit, no? Humor aside, it was a very lovely evening, and I could see how special this tradition was in their household. I was happy to have witnessed it, but I did not feel a part of it. I gained no ground in finding a religion, just the number of a great Chinese vegan take-out restaurant and the conclusion that perhaps the most Jewish thing about me was my affinity for Chinese food.

Next up was Prince of Peace Episcopal Church. Ahhhh, *Catholic Lite*. Great taste, less Pope. This church was close to home, so it earned points in the "geographically desirable" category. Plus, my good friend goes there, so I didn't have to go by myself. We went to the eight o'clock service. Much less crowded than the ten o'clock. In fact, it was really not very full at all. I think I was at least twenty years younger than ninety-five percent of the people there. It felt a bit like I was at a retirement center. Everyone seemed very friendly, though. I got the impression that most of the folks knew each other. The sermon was short in length and rather short on content, too. I don't actually remember what it was about. A few hymns were peppered in—hymns I'd never heard before and, from the sounds of the mumbled voices of the congregants, hymns *they*'d never heard before either.

To be fair, I think that there probably is a lot more oomph to the ten o'clock service. I noticed that one of the priests had dozed off at some point, his head at first seemingly nodded in prayer, but then every few minutes it would jerk up suddenly and then drift down again as sleep overtook him. My friend told me that he'd been very ill and hadn't been in church for a while. She was glad to see him up there, even if he was sleeping. Good thing this was "Catholic Lite" and not straight up hard-core Catholic. I imagine that some mean nun would have bounded on up to slap his hands with a ruler if this had happened during mass.

I was far too fascinated by the bobbing head of the robed man in the fancy chair on stage to pay any attention to the younger robed man at the pulpit. The only thing that really caught my interest was his plea for donations for a missionary school in Uganda. Apparently prayers had been answered and a corporation had generously offered to double any money donated by the church to this very needy and deserving school. Men in robes singing warbley hymns were not my thing, but give me poor kids in Uganda and I'm all ears. I didn't need to imagine these thin brown children eager to learn to read and write. No, I didn't need to imagine them because there they were, in bright vivid color photographs on brochures at the table in the court-yard after the service was over.

It seemed that while we were in there praying and singing (and some of us sleeping), the courtyard had magically transformed into a makeshift marketplace. There were displays for various missionary endeavors, the Ugandan school being one, and for donations for Christmas gifts for our own local needy. The church was collecting new and gently used bicycles and helmets. They even had someone there who was a wiz at fixing up old bikes. This was quite impressive. I liked how these church people were focused on helping others. But Episcopalianism wasn't for me. I hadn't found what I was looking for. I did, however, write a check to the school in Uganda.

. . . .

I was beginning to think I was destined to church shop for the rest of my life when a friend of mine from kickboxing invited me to go along with her and her sister to "church." I explained to her that I was currently in the process of looking for a spiritual home and so the timing was perfect. I did think it was odd that her church con-vened on Fridays instead of on Sundays, like most of them do. But she's Mexican American and so I assumed she was Catholic and that perhaps there was some special Mass or something that took place on Friday afternoons.

"Then you *have* to come to church with us!" She said with a mischievous grin. "You should know that Vicki and I pray to the

Patrón Saint. You know . . . as in *St. Margarita*. We go every Friday." Now this was an offer I couldn't refuse. Turns out that going to church had a whole different meaning to them than it did to everybody else; for them it meant getting together for a big Mexican feast and shots of tequila. They do it every Friday. Religiously. That sounded like fun to me, so I met up with them a couple of hours later at a darling little white stucco "church," also known as the Adobe Cantina. The girls were already seated on the patio when I arrived looking very un-churchlady-like, each with a large margarita and a basket of chips to share. It's kind of like communion, right?

"I'll have what they're having," I called to the waiter. He came back with another margarita and three shots of tequila. We ordered a few plates of food to share, and as our drinks went down the mood went up. Our sermon to each other was full of good gossip, war stories about motherhood, crazy exes, cousins, stepchildren, etc. Confession is good for the soul. And lobster tacos are absolutely divine for the taste buds. Our "service" lasted over two hours, and when it was over, I felt really uplifted. It may not have been in a stained glass cathedral or anything, but it definitely made me feel included, cared for, listened to, and loved. And if that ain't what church is about, I don't know what is.

I had set out to find *one* place of worship, *one* true religion, but in the end, I realized that for me, at least for now, that wasn't necessary. I'm not saying that I don't believe in a higher power, it's just that I don't really think I can choose one religion over another. It's not because they are apples and oranges, it's because they are all ice cream. Before you think that the tequila from my last worship experience hasn't worn off, let me explain. The things I liked about all religions are the things they have in common, and boy do they have a lot in common. It didn't matter what the various religions called God, or whether they followed the Old Testament, the New Testament, or any other good book—and that includes the menu at the Adobe Cantina. They all shared the belief that there was a greater power, that it was important to love one another, help one another, and try to live a good and purposeful life. They're like ice cream—all good, just different flavors. Why should I have to stick to just one?

When I put "go church shopping" on my list, I set out to discover what was true for me, and that is exactly what I did. I can find my brotherhood anywhere and everywhere I look—in a church, in a synagogue, in the home of friends, in online chat rooms, in a Mexican restaurant even. I started out uncomfortable with the fact that I was a mutt. Now I am proud of it. In a way, I came full circle and returned to that old Unitarian Universalist sentiment that I am indeed *okay*, you are *okay*, and that is more than *okay* with me.

~~#10 Go church shopping (pick a religion, any religion)~~

. . . .

There was another challenge on my list that had to do with religion, or more specifically, with the Ten Commandments. The one about honoring one's mother and father resonated with me, and so I set out to do just that. I wanted to do something that would really speak to their character, reflect who they are and what they stand for. This challenge would be about them, not me. Well, that's not really true, it was still about me. Everything on my list is about me. That was kind of the whole point of the list in the first place. But, as had happened with so many of the things on that list, it became not so much about the task itself as it was about the process of doing it.

Since my parents are alive I was able to talk to them about what they'd like me to do to honor them. My father and stepmother liked the idea of a donation being made to the Children's Institute, an amazing facility in Pittsburgh that I hope no one reading this will ever have to see. It's a place where children suffering from disease, a disorder, or a very bad injury go to recover. They have many specialists on staff and great around-the-clock medical care. My family came to know the institute well after my half-sister, Anne, was in a car accident in January 2001, when she was only sixteen.

Anne had agreed to go with her friend, Rachel, to buy new jazz shoes on one condition: Rachel, who was driving, had to take her through the drive-through at Wendy's to get something to eat. Rachel took a short cut, which involved having to cross a very busy one-way, multilane street to get to a little alley that led to Wendy's. They almost made it, too. But about three-quarters of the way across that busy street a truck came speeding around the bend. There were buses lined up along the curb, which I'm sure blocked both the truck driver's and Rachel's view of each other until it was too late. The truck drove straight into the passenger side, where Anne was sitting. It was a state-owned vehicle, not a little pickup truck, and so its force pushed the car about thirty feet against the grain of the tires and into a pole.

Miraculously, Rachel sustained little injury. Anne was unconscious. After she was extracted from the car with the Jaws of Life the paramedics did a series of tests using the Glasgow Coma Scale. They checked things like spontaneous respiration (she didn't have any), response to pain (she didn't move when they jabbed her in the sternum with an instrument), and whether her pupils dilated and refracted with light. That last one was the only thing she had going for her. They assign a score based on the results of that test, and, generally, the higher your score on a scale of one to ten, the better your chances of a good outcome. Anne scored a three.

She was taken to the University of Pittsburgh Medical Center, which is a really good teaching hospital. My father had been brought to the scene by a neighbor and rode in the ambulance with Anne. Once they arrived she was whisked away on a gurney and my dad had to wait there, not knowing what was happening. What did end up happening was that the doctor had to drill holes in Anne's skull and put shunts into her ventricles to drain fluid from her rapidly swelling brain.

She also had three broken vertebrae, a collapsed lung, a lacerated kidney, and a broken pelvis. The doctors didn't mention any of this to the family because Anne was in a coma and not moving, and she was not necessarily going to make it through the next forty-eight hours. With a brain injury like the one Anne had, the swelling continues to go up for as long as forty-eight hours before it starts to come down. And if it goes up too much, and there is nowhere for the brain to go, the patient does not live. This was going to be the longest forty-eight hours of any of our lives. "Wait and see" are three of the most horrible words in the English language.

When I got the call about Anne's accident I was home alone with the kids. Feeling very helpless and useless in Los Angeles, I jumped on a flight to Pittsburgh to join my parents in the waiting room of the neurological intensive care unit. We just sat there. Waiting. Nothing can prepare you to see a loved one look so, so fragile, and so, so broken. Her beautiful red hair had been partially shaved and there were those holes in her head with the tubes draining brain fluid. She had a central line and was hooked to a ventilator. She still was not breathing on her own, nor would she for quite some time.

Ultimately, Anne did come back to us, but it was not like in the movies where a person in a coma just wakes up and is completely lucid and coherent, not by a long shot. She would open her eyes and look around, but she didn't seem to recognize any of us. She also was flailing her arms and legs around. "Nonpurposeful movement" they call it. We'd ask her to squeeze our hands and sometimes she would do it, and sometimes she would not. It was hard to know exactly how much she understood.

She was moved to the Children's Institute, where she began her very difficult road to recovery. She'd been given a tracheostomy, so there was a hole in her neck with a tube attached to the ventilator, and she also had feeding tubes. She'd lost alot of weight and looked like a skeleton. She was in diapers. I'd changed her many times when she was a baby, but I never thought I'd do it when she was a teenager. Still, she had survived. "Wait and see" now meant wait and see what she might regain. Whether she would breathe on her own, swallow on her own, walk on her own, speak. At one point the nurses said a good goal for her might be to comb her own hair. It's amazing how much we take for granted, and how something like this can really put the world into perspective.

Anne worked with occupational therapists, speech therapists, and physical therapists every day. Little by little, she seemed to improve. She got off of the ventilator. She was able to swallow. And finally, she spoke. You know what her first words were? "Can I have a small Sprite?"

It took months and months of concerted effort on Anne's part, and prayer, persistence, and perseverance on the whole family's part, but she did come out the other side of that nightmare. She had to relearn so many things, including how to comb her hair. But in the end, she did make an excellent recovery in large part due to the wonderful staff at the Children's Institute. That place had become a second home for my folks, and so it was the first thing that came to mind when I asked my question. They have so much in the way of therapies and equipment, but still, they need more. With my father and stepmother's approval, I sent a monetary gift in their name to honor them. I was grateful for being able to help the institute, especially on behalf of people they have helped so much. Anne went on to earn her Masters in education and has followed in her mother's footsteps and become a teacher. She's married now and living in Chicago. Who knows what wonderful things life has in store for her. I guess we'll just have to wait and see.

. . . .

Coming up with something to honor my mother was not as simple, as she is involved in quite a few causes. I called her up and explained what I was doing and why I was doing it. She was really excited. "I'm pretty hot on politics," she said. This did not come as news to me. As long as I can remember she's been "hot on politics."

Her mother was very involved in politics also, as are most people on that side of our family. My mom volunteered for the Democratic party long before she had us kids, and she always stayed involved and informed. I don't think she was quite as active when she was raising us, as she was also going to med school and then working as a physician. But after retiring, she moved to San Diego and has served as a Precinct Leader, the Regional Coordinator for the GO Team (Grassroots Organizing Team), and on the Executive Board for the San Diego County Democratic Party.

She told me about an organization called "Southern Poverty Law Center" which was founded by Morris Dees. "He's my hero!" my mom exclaimed. Not only did I not know that Morris Dees was my mother's hero, I had no idea who Morris Dees was. I'd never heard her mention him, but then again, I'd never asked her about this kind of thing. The organization was created for the purpose of fulfilling the promises of the civil rights movement.

My mom reminded me (again) that she'd marched with Dr. King in 1963 and that she'd heard him deliver that famous "I Have a Dream" speech. "I'd like you to do something to further the Civil Rights cause," she requested. "Look up the Southern Poverty Law Center. They're online." After perusing their site, it did seem that they had been very diligent in advocating reform and education, both aiding victims of discrimination and teaching children to "embrace diversity" and "respect differences," which in turn helps ensure a more peaceful future for generations to come. This was the perfect cause to support in honor of my mom.

#11 Do something to honor my parents

. . . .

I decided to extend the commandment about honoring parents to include grandparents as well. Mine had all passed away, so I couldn't ask them how they would've wanted to be honored. I had to think of something personal, something that would reflect who they were, so that others might be touched by their kindness and come to know what they stood for.

If there was ever anyone more involved in politics than my mother, it would have to have been Grandma Joan. She was the Vice Chair for Kennedy's campaign in Colorado. The Chair was Byron White, who subsequently became a Supreme Court Justice. My grandmother should have been appointed Director of the Denver Mint, or so the story goes. But she wasn't and ended up taking a job with B'nai B'rith Women in Washington, D.C., instead. My mom says that Grandma really should have gotten that appointment, but in the end it was for the best that she didn't. After Kennedy was shot, Johnson let go a lot of the people the late president had appointed, so my grandmother most likely would've been out of a job. And, of course, if she hadn't moved to D.C., then my mother would not have applied to George Washington University and wouldn't have met my father and I would never have been born. File that under *everything for a reason.*

My grandmother was the membership director for B'nai B'rith Women for many years. She was working there when terrorists took over the building in 1977. I remember answering the phone one day and my grandmother was on the other end telling me in a whisper, "Just in case your mother is watching television right now, tell her not to worry. I'm fine. I can't talk now because they'll see the line lit up on the phone." And then she hung up. When I relayed the message to my mother, she immediately flipped on the TV and saw that terrorists were attacking my grandmother's building. My grandmother and a bunch of her co-workers were hiding in one of the offices.

I know I should remember which terrorist group it was that held my grandmother hostage, how long they were in there, whether anybody got killed, and how the standoff finally ended. But all I remember is my grandmother's hushed voice on the other end of the telephone. That, and the fact that she and the other people hiding with her used a wastepaper basket as a toilet. What can I say? I was seven.

Grandma Joan was a lifetime member of B'nai B'rith Women, a gift from her children that came with a gold charm. The charm outlasted the organization. B'nai B'rith Women was a politically conscious Jewish women's organization that campaigned for issues like free choice in abortion, equal Social Security benefits for women, and women's healthcare. It later was renamed Jewish Women International. My mother said as much as Grandma loved B'nai B'rith, she probably wouldn't want me to make a donation to them in her honor, as the Anti-Defamation League is now part of that organization. They'd come out against the building of the mosque in New York near Ground Zero, and Grandma was all for religious freedom.

She also was a big fan of education. She used to volunteer at an elementary school in a low-income neighborhood in D.C., teaching literacy to kids and also to adults. Her love of teaching extended to her grandchildren; our visits with her always included trips to the many museums in D.C., as well as outings to the Kennedy Center and days spent working as volunteers in the White House. I didn't realize it at the time, but not all children spend vacations collating papers and stuffing envelopes for the President. Because of her involvement, I attended Carter's inauguration. I was so little, though, that all I remember of it was rolling on a grassy hill. I never really gave much thought as to how special it was to have had the opportunity to volunteer in the White House and attend a presidential inauguration. That is, until I started thinking about how to honor my grandmother.

My grandmother volunteered in the White House on a regular basis during all of the Democratic presidents' terms. Even in her eighties, she answered the opinion lines for President Clinton. She worked diligently for the Woman's National Democratic Club, and that was the last place she worked for the party. I decided—and my mother concurred—that doing something for "The Club" (as my grandparents called it) would be the best choice.

"If only she could have lived to see Obama elected," my mom said. "She would have been thrilled." Even though she'd already passed, her influence was still evident in Obama's campaign and presidency. His campaign manager and chief advisor is my second cousin once removed David Axelrod. My grandmother and his mother Myril (who we know as Cousin Mitzi) were first cousins. The two of them were raised like sisters, and they spent a lot of time with each other's children. The story goes that my grandmother had a big influence on David, and that she was more than encouraging in his choice to pursue a career in politics. And if that isn't enough, my first cousin Tamara Cofman Wittes (my mother's sister's daughter) held the post of Deputy Assistant Secretary for Near Eastern Affairs at the United States Department of State. So, my grandmother's legacy lives on.

For a while my cousin Tammy's parents lived in Turkey for my then Uncle Don's work (he and my Aunt Becky later divorced).

When Grandma Joan was there for a visit they went to a diplomatic reception and that's where she met Grandpa Bruce. He was really my *step*grandfather. But they were married when I was only a few months old, so to me he was my grandfather. I knew he'd worked for the government, and I discovered that Grandpa Bruce went to Turkey as the representative to the CENTO secretariat.

"Grandpa Bruce used to work as a labor organizer for the Congress of Industrial Organizations, the CIO," my mom explained. This led to a little history lesson as to how the CIO merged with the American Federation of Labor, but before this, the CIO was strictly for blue-collar workers. Grandpa Bruce had been sent down South to organize labor. After that, he was a civil servant. He was the Assistant to the Assistant to the Secretary of State for Labor and the labor attaché for many U.S. embassies, including India, Norway, Italy, and Turkey. "He wrote a book!" my mom said. It's called *The Political Role of Labor in Developing Countries.*

My grandparents had a wonderful relationship. They were always supportive of one another's interests. For example, my grandfather was very involved at the Woman's National Democratic Club. I knew doing something to honor my grandparents together would have made them very happy. And so I am now an official member of "The Club" and the proud donor of a brick in their garden wall with a plaque that reads, "In Loving Memory of Joan and Bruce Millen."

My biological maternal grandfather was Grandpa David. My mother's parents were divorced when she was in high school and her dad remained in Colorado after her mom moved to D.C. Though my mom says Grandpa David spent time with us kids when we were young, I have little memory of it. I remember visiting him and his wife, Rita, one time. They lived in a mobile home, which fascinated me. Grandpa David always had a cigar dangling from his mouth and a couple of Chihuahuas following him everywhere, even into the bathroom. I was ten when Grandpa David died. I was the one who had to tell my mother, because she'd been out when the call came. I didn't realize the gravity of what I was saying to her. Shortly after that I won a goldfish at a local fair. I named him David.

I guess to ten-year-old me it was a good way to honor my grandfather. Thirty years later I came to the same conclusion. I Googled "Animal Shelter Pueblo, Colorado" and found a slew of articles about a new facility being built by Paws for Life. They'd just had their groundbreaking ceremony and construction had begun on a state-of-the-art, no-kill facility to shelter Pueblo's homeless animals. The timing couldn't have been better. I contacted them via e-mail and they quickly responded. They were so excited that news of their project had reached California. They had various different "naming" opportunities that included benches, fencing, fountains, landscaping, etc. I opted to make a general donation in my Grandpa David's name and am proud to honor his memory in doing so.

Then I turned my attention to my father's parents, my Grandma and Grandpa Campbell. They lived closer to us, in Aliquippa, PA, so I saw them more often. They were a lot older than my mother's parents. They'd had my father rather late in life for that generation; my grandmother was forty-two when he was born. This was my Methodist side, and my grandparents were pillars of their church in Aliquippa. When my grandmother was very old, in her late nineties, she told me the story of how she became a Methodist. I'd always thought that she was born that way, but no, she'd been raised Presbyterian. She said that when she and my grandfather were courting they used to walk up the hill together on Sundays, then she would turn left into the Presbyterian Church, and he would turn right into the Methodist church. Once they were married they walked up that hill and when he turned right, she turned and followed him. Just like that. No discussion, no question, she just turned right instead of left and from that day forward she was a Methodist.

And what a Methodist she was. She loved that church and all the people in it. She was a Sunday school teacher and might have been on the board of directors, but she was a woman and therefore disallowed. She was an officer of the Women's Society of Christian Service and served as secretary for many years.

Grandpa Jim was also very active in the running of the church. He used to wake up very early every Sunday morning and get the furnace going so that the church would be warm when the rest of the congregants arrived. That's how he was, very quiet and strong, dedicated, and humble. He never wanted any recognition for what he did, he just felt good doing it, and that was enough. He died of emphysema when I was thirteen. Ironically, he never smoked a day in his life. It must have been all the years he worked in the steel mill. My grandmother outlived him by twenty years. When she passed away at the age of 100, we had a luncheon at that church after her funeral. It was wonderful to see the many old photographs of my grandparents hanging on the walls.

Thinking of the two of them, imagining them walking together that Sunday, both turning right instead of parting ways at the top of that hill, made me smile. I knew that they would have been honored if I did something to continue their strong commitment to the church they both called their spiritual home, The First United Methodist Church of Aliquippa. And so, I made a financial contribution in their name to be used as the church sees fit. I also sent a check to the American Lung Association to help fight emphysema and other respiratory diseases.

I wish I had thought to honor my grandparents sooner. I'd have loved to talk with them about what they would have liked me to do for them. But talking to my parents was the next best thing. All it took was that one question, "What do you think I could do that would honor your parents?" And the floodgates opened. All sorts of stories poured out, stories that I had never heard before. In taking on this challenge of honoring my parents and grandparents, I was aiming to practice religion. Since I myself wasn't going to be any one religion or another, I chose something from the Ten Commandments, a set of rules for living a good life that most religions seemed to subscribe to. Yes, I set out to honor my parents, and grandparents, but in the end I was the one who was honored. Honored to be able to do something for them, honored to get to know more about them, and honored to be a part of such a rich and interesting history. I learned a lot of their stories, which only added to my own.

When you are making your own list, you might want to include something that involves family. In learning about your family's past, you can trace a path to where you are today, and I'm not just talking geography. Does your family have any unusual traditions? Do you know the story of how your ancestors got to this country and why they came here? Why did they leave where they came from? There are all kinds of dramatic events that you might not even know about but which have affected aspects of your life and influenced how you were raised and how you live your life today. You might consider making a family tree, investigating the origins of a family tradition, or simply interviewing your parents, grandparents, cousins, aunts, and uncles about their lives. These stories are rarely boring. You don't have to do anything specifically to "honor your mother and father," or grandparents either for that matter, although I am pretty certain that your taking an interest in them will honor them plenty.

#12 Do something to honor my grandparents

. . . .

At the beginning of this chapter I asked the question, "Are you there, God?" and I'd put "go church shopping (pick a religion, any religion)" on my list in order to find out the answer. Well, turns out the answer was, "Yes." In my search for God I was prepared to knock on many doors. I was not prepared, however, to find Him behind every single one of them. And yes, that includes the door to the Adobe Cantina.

I knocked and He answered. It was not at all like one of those game shows where you have to pick the *right* door in order to win the prize. For me at least, they were all right doors. They may have looked different on the outside, but inside they were surprisingly the same. Turns out, I didn't have to pick a religion after all. I was free to embrace my spirituality and know that I belonged to a universal truth that cannot be divided. And since that's the case, I am not really *half* Jewish or *half* Methodist. I am wholly (and holy) me. Honoring my parents and grandparents was my way of embracing that fact. Learning about them taught me so much about myself. I do not *half* belong to each side of my family. I fully belong to both.

As you create your list, think about whether or not there is some aspect of yourself that you might feel is not clear or defined. For me it was religion, but for you it might be something else. It's as good a time as any to discover what your own personal truth is. Take the time to get to know yourself, find out what is important to you, what is meaningful to you, and then, if it isn't what you thought it would be, that's okay. If you can set aside your expectations about the truth, your beliefs about the truth, and what others have told you to believe about it, you will be able to focus simply on *the truth itself*, you will get that clarity you are searching for.

FIVE

STAR OF STAGE AND SCREEN

A s you come up with ideas for your list, certain things will set off a negative voice in your head. This voice will no doubt try to talk you out of writing down X, Y, or Z. Don't pay attention to it, though, because it's just your fear trying to keep you from taking chances. If you sit quietly and concentrate, you'll start to hear a different voice, one that is positive. Unfortunately, it's also a lot quieter. But if you listen closely, it will tell you what the list should include. Write everything down with complete abandon.

When you're finished, look for common themes. I'm sure you'll find some. For example, when I finished writing my own list I noticed there were quite a few things on it that had to do with performing. Was that a coincidence? Hardly. The common themes are there for a reason; they reveal clues about yourself that you must investigate. These clues are like puzzle pieces. For me, it wasn't until I'd crossed all of the performance goals off of my list that the pieces started falling into place.

My fascination with the spotlight started very early. As a child, I fantasized about becoming a trapeze artist, and I also wanted to sing, dance, act—the whole shebang. If it involved applause, I wanted to do it. I'm sure there are more than a few of you reading this who also practiced your Oscar acceptance speech in front of the mirror. I loved to sing and dance and make up plays. Very quickly I realized that grown-ups give heaps of attention to cute little kids who perform, and so I performed as often as I could, at the drop of a hat. It became my favorite way to feed my need for attention and approval.

I was like one of those laboratory mice that ran through the maze in order to get the cheese. Over the course of my life my confidence has risen and fallen. My ability to perform well seemed dependent upon external encouragement, or cheese, if you will. And while I hadn't performed at all in a very long time, I could not deny that the dream was still alive. Otherwise, why would I have included so many performance-related things on my list? Without really knowing what I hoped to gain, I set out to conquer them all—be in a stage show, take guitar lessons, and get a paid acting job.

. . . .

You know that saying, "All the world is a stage?" When I was little I took it literally. I sang and danced in restaurants and stores, on busses and subways, airplanes, and, of course, at home in my living room. I covered all the popular music of the day. In kindergarten I did a mean version of Captain & Tennille's 1975 hit "Love Will Keep Us Together." I sang it at recess, standing up on a low brick wall. On a good day a couple of kids would cluster around and watch my impromptu show. On a *great* day a teacher would notice and call other teachers over: "Come take a look at this! Little Susan Campbell is singing "Love Will Keep Us Together"! How on earth did she learn all the words?" they'd say in disbelief.

How did I learn the words? By listening to the song over and over and over and over again, that's how. Which meant my family had to listen to the song over and over and over and over again, too. No matter. They would thank me later when I was a star, I thought. I had a hairbrush with a ballerina painted on the back that made the perfect microphone. As I grew older, I figured out ways to up the ante. I turned my cousins into backup singers, changed up lyrics to fit special occasions, and, perhaps most important, I read my audience. No grandmother (or friend of said grandmother) wants to see her precious granddaughter shake her hips to "That's the Way (uh huh, uh huh) I Like It," but give them "You Light up My Life" and they melt like butter.

I kept on with the whole "cute little kid singing for quarters" shtick until I was no longer a cute little kid. By then my parents were divorced and the main adults in my life, my regular audience, were otherwise occupied. Nobody was in the mood for my song-and-dance routine, and my confidence sank. My desire for attention and approval, however, did not. Neediness and nervousness are the two main ingredients of a perfume called desperation, and if middle school girls pick up that scent on you, you're doomed. I reeked of it. My one good friend deserted me for a pack of these girls, and the group of them seemed bent on making my first year at Florence Reizenstein Middle School a living hell. They did not like me, so I felt unlikeable. They called me fat and ugly, and there was not a mirror in the world that could convince me otherwise. Looking back now at the few photos I have of myself at that age, I can see that I was quite thin and fairly cute for being in the throes of the awkward early teen years. But I didn't feel that way at the time.

Needless to say, I was an emotional mess. This did not bode well for me when tryouts rolled around for the annual junior high musical at the Jewish Community Center. In spite of the fact that the girls who'd been harassing me were all going to be there, I tried out. I was scared to death when it was my turn to audition. We lined up in the hallway and waited to be called into a room one at a time to sing a song of our choosing in front of a small handful of grown-ups. When it was my turn, my throat became so tight that my voice was barely audible. I was not at all surprised that I wound up in the chorus.

I went to rehearsals and tried to stay clear of my tormentors. They all had bigger parts and seemed pretty occupied with learning their lines, as well as the songs and dances. I, who had dreamed of being a big star, spent most of my time trying not to be noticed. Eventually the trouble with those girls dissipated, but my confidence remained shaken. Regardless, throughout the rest of middle school and high school I took dance lessons and tried out for a couple of musicals, but my auditions didn't improve so I was always cast in some obscure role, like Orphan #6. This continued throughout high school, right up until the senior class play. It was *Guys and Dolls*, and I was cast as a Hot Box Dancer. Unfortunately, Hot Box Dancer was simply another way to say "member of the chorus."

When I went to college I found a whole new audience: sorority sisters. These girls were supportive and encouraging, I was singing again and, more important at the time, I received approval and applause. I sang in chapter meetings; I sang in rush skits; I even joined a gospel choir.

College afforded me some great opportunities to perform. But out in the working world there are no talent shows or rush skits. At least not at the advertising agency I worked for. My singing was relegated to the shower once again, until I had kids. I sang to my children from the day they were born. I learned all the words to the songs from their favorite Disney movies. These songs became a part of their bedtime ritual. Sometimes I would find myself in their rooms, singing away, long after they had conked out. It wasn't until they were older that I sang in front of someone who was not related to me, asleep, or both.

In 2005, we moved to Hidden Hills, California, the land of horses and divorces (that's what the horse-loving divorcées call it, anyway). Hidden Hills does have its fair share of horses and divorces, but it also has quite a few actors and a community theater. It's used mostly for children's productions, but once a year the more theatrical adult members of the community put on a show. Valentine's Day weekend the theater is reserved for four of the silliest, raunchiest performances you could ever hope to see. And all the proceeds go to charity. When I added "perform on stage in a play or musical" to my list, I knew exactly how to make that happen.

The shows are open to any resident who wants to participate, though an audition is required. The audition consists of stopping by the home of the couple that directs the show each year and singing something while the husband accompanies you on piano. You can choose any song in any key (as long as he knows it or has the sheet music). Simple right? No matter how badly you sing, you're automatically in the show in some capacity. Nonetheless, before my audition the butterflies were having their way with me.

I had flashbacks to my Jewish Community Center junior high musical days. I wanted it to be different this time. I wanted to have the spotlight back—recapture a little of my "Love Will Keep Us Together" fame. I practiced singing several different songs, and finally settled on one of my all-time favorites, "There Are Worse Things I Could Do." It's the song Rizzo sings in *Grease*, a musical David Frank had once been the conductor of on Broadway. Who is David Frank? The guy who was sitting at the piano waiting to accompany me, that's who.

What were the chances? "I should have Googled him!" I thought to myself, but it was too late, he had already started playing it on the piano. Fortunately, this time I didn't choke; my throat didn't tighten as it had in my middle school audition catastrophes. I sounded pretty darn good, in fact. Not amazing, not perfect, but good enough that I was assigned a solo, and I've had a solo part every year since. While I'm not the best singer of the bunch (not by a long shot), I hold my own.

What changed? Was it all the practice hours I'd logged in singing to the kids? Maybe. But it wasn't just my voice that was stronger. It was my confidence. My desire to perform on that Hidden Hills stage was less about approval and more about my desire to perform. I was able to enjoy the experience, the thrill of entertaining. I was communicating with the audience and making them happier. I appreciated their applause, but it was no longer my goal.

#13 ~~Perform on stage in a play or musical~~

. . . .

Acting in a musical theater production was the first item on my list that had to do with performing, but it was not the last. I had also written down "take guitar lessons." Musical ability runs in my family. Well, it runs on my father's side of my family. Tone deafness seems to run on my mother's side. My father sings nicely, and he can play almost any instrument by ear. His sister Ardele was a real prodigy, she played piano like an angel. (At least according to my grandmother she did.) She received a music scholarship from Oberlin.

When I was young, we inherrited an old upright piano, but neither my sister nor I were encouraged to play. We weren't discouraged either, though, and so we started playing by ear. We could hammer out "Chopsticks," "Heart and Soul," and a few other tunes. It wasn't until I was five and we moved to Pittsburgh that my sister and I had lessons. Elizabeth took it seriously, learning to read the sheet music the teacher put in front of her and practicing every day. I on the other hand, hated piano lessons. My mother let me off the hook. Why pay for lessons for someone who clearly didn't want them.

Truth of the matter was that I longed to be able to play, but I wanted to be able to play perfectly, right that minute. I was accustomed to playing real songs using both hands, but finding out that I wasn't playing the correct notes or positioning my hands properly on the keyboard was a slap in the face. I'd thought it would be easy. But the notes on the pages meant nothing to me and the songs the teacher gave me to play were for babies. I didn't want to be struggling through "Twinkle Twinkle Little Star" when my sister was playing Mozart. I also didn't want to hear the speech about patience and about how Elizabeth was three years older than I was, and so I should not expect to be able to play the way she could. Before the lessons, we were equal. We were equally bad, but still equal. Now she was better. So I quit the piano. There were a gazillion other instruments out there and surely I would be better than her at one of them.

A year or so after my parents divorced, my mother signed Elizabeth and me up for a day camp for the arts. It was held at Chatham College, which had beautiful grounds and old buildings. I took all kinds of classes there. I tried a lot of different instruments: the violin, the viola, the cello, the harp, and drums, and while I liked them all, I didn't really love any of them. I wasn't particularly good at any of them, either. I took the fact that I couldn't sit down and play perfectly to mean that I would never be able to play at all. It was less painful to quit than to find out I was right.

A couple of years later, my father was remarried to a woman who was very musically gifted in her own right, my stepmother, Margie. She was the choir director at her Catholic church and taught middle school music. Her father, Bill, was also a singer and loved to tell stories about when he was a medic and also in the Army band during WWII. He had even performed with Bob Hope! It was my new stepmother's stepfather, Joe, however, who really got me interested in playing an instrument again. Every summer we spent a week or two with Joe and Mary Jo (my stepmother's mother) at their home in Delaware. Joe played a variety of instruments and was really excited to have "grandchildren" to share that with, even if we were double-step-grandchildren. He taught me some basic chords and let me strum his guitar while he picked out tunes on his banjo. We donned bright-colored bandanas on our heads and performed after dinner every night. We called it the "Gypsy Joe Show."

I was so inspired by my performances with Joe, I bought an old Stella steel stringed guitar at a yard sale and began to try and teach myself. My mother was happy to see signs that I might stick with an instrument, and bought me a really nice Guild acoustic guitar for my birthday. While I couldn't put my finger on it at the time, her gift created an unspoken expectation (in my mind, at least) that I'd start learning to play guitar in earnest. The fact that real money had been invested made me feel pressured to put in time and master more chords and songs. It was no longer fun. Aside from summer Gypsy Joe Shows at my step-grandparents', I did not play; that beautiful new acoustic guitar stayed in its case.

Looking back now I realize that my fear of not living up to expectations, or more accurately, what I *imagined* others' expectations to be, had overtaken my interest in learning to play. I could never bring myself to get rid of that guitar, but every time I looked at it I was reminded of one more thing that I might have been good at, but that I had chickened out of giving a fair shot.

When my own kids were small, I bought a used baby grand piano. It sat unplayed but looked awfully nice in my living room. My kids instead developed an interest in electric guitar. I wanted them to start with acoustic, but they would have none of it. If they were going to take lessons there would have to be an amplifier involved.

We made a trip to the Guitar Center and hired a teacher who would come to the house once a week to give lessons.

I could hear the kids laughing and having fun, the teacher letting them choose which songs they wanted to tackle and giving them space to "riff" and be creative. I was trying to enjoy this experience vicariously through them, which, of course, is impossible. It wasn't long before I decided to "take guitar lessons"—a goal from my list. When I dug my old Guild out of the storage closet, I discovered that while the case was dusty, my old guitar was as beautiful as ever, minus a couple of broken strings. The guitar teacher took it with him when he left and brought it back restrung, tuned, and as good as new. The little I did know I hadn't forgotten and, by the end of my first lesson I'd learned two more songs: REO Speedwagon's "Heard it From a Friend" and the Eagles' "Hotel California." I feel absolutely no pressure to keep taking lessons. I was playing for the fun of it. I'm happy to sit in my living room now and play on a rainy day when nobody is home to listen but the dogs.

#14 ~~Take guitar lessons~~

. . . .

Crossing two of my performing goals off of my list was a huge confidence booster. Furthermore, I was starting to really enjoy performing for performing's sake—no audience necessary, no Type A urge to practice enough to win a Tony or Grammy. Enjoying something is enough of a reason to do it, and what other people think or expect should have no bearing on whether or not I choose to sing, dance, play guitar, or stand on my head. Looking back now I think that may have been the lesson I needed to learn, and the ultimate reason behind why there were so many performance-related challenges on my list. But it wasn't until after I'd completed them all that I figured that out. Still on my list was #16: "get a paid acting job." The fact that it had to be paid should have been a gigantic red flag that I was still desperately seeking outside approval.

The fear of never getting that approval is what had kept me from pursuing acting as an adult, but my senior year of college I found a way to test the waters without the risk of failing. I signed up for a scene study class that was graded on a pass/no pass basis. All I had to do was show up; there would be no expectations whatsoever, so I didn't have to be good. The plan was that if anyone mocked me, I would simply say that I signed up on a dare. My teacher—I wish I could remember his name—was very encouraging. In our second class we had to improvise getting ready for bed. I brushed my teeth in front of everybody and was very believable. Either that or the teacher was easily impressed. Regardless, I stayed in the course and really enjoyed it. But that was never enough of a reason for me to do anything, and this was no different.

As much as I liked acting in that safe environment: no auditions, no audience, no grades, I didn't consider signing up for another. I stuck to my writing courses, and in 1991 I graduated cum laude, moved to Los Angeles, and took a job with an advertising agency. I wanted to be a real writer, not a copywriter, but I also didn't want to starve. I figured I'd get a job as a copywriter writing those clever television commercials by day and write the great American novel/screenplay/collection of short stories by night. Well, that didn't happen either. I quickly found out that you couldn't just walk into an ad agency and get a job as a copywriter; it's not exactly an entry-level position. I did manage to land a job at an ad agency: Executive Assistant. That was my official title. My unofficial title was "Peon Who Did Whatever Chore That the Sr. Account Executive Couldn't Get the Junior Account Executive Who Couldn't Get the Assistant Account Executive to Do."

There were very few perks with that job (as I'm sure you can imagine), but there was one good thing about it. A friend, Brittany Marley, who'd been hired at the same time I was worked as a peon in the media department. I knew Brittany from San Diego, where we'd lived in the same condo complex while attending different universities. She and her then husband had moved to Los Angeles so he could pursue his dream of becoming an actor, just like everybody else. One time, Brittany was watching one of her favorite shows when a message flashed on the television screen. They had a phone number to call to win a chance at appearing in a promotion for the show. She called, and when they called her back with an audition time she was thrilled! Her husband, who would have given anything to book an audition, was less than thrilled. He would not agree to go with her, and so I did.

I'd never seen this show and really was just there as moral support. But when the casting director saw me he asked me to audition as well. It was to be a testimonial type of spot—real people in natural settings talking about how amazing this show was. The one I had never seen. I explained that to the guy but he said not to worry, he'd tell me what to say. Lo and behold, both my friend and I were picked. At the shoot they dressed me in a floral outfit and arranged me on a garden bench. Sure, totally natural. I waxed on and on about this show (which by now I'd learned at least the premise of) and they made not one, but two commercials out of it, which aired nationally on ABC. I'd been paid the standard going rate for a day of acting work, but I would have done it for free—that's how much I loved it.

I attended workshops at night to put together my junior portfolio and continued along the path toward becoming a copywriter, but my plan had changed a bit. Now I was going to work as a copywriter (in order not to starve), write the great American novel/screenplay/collection of short stories *and* become a famous actor. The idea of it sounded great, but I did nothing at all to proceed in that direction. Except for the first part. I was hired as a copywriter by the first ad agency I sent my portfolio. I didn't write the great American novel, or any other novel for that matter, and I had no clue how to get an acting career going. Apparently it isn't every day that one gets asked to audition just by sitting around.

I decided to be proactive and take an acting class. So what if it was a soap opera acting class taught by a name-dropping nobody who probably had zero connections. It was a baby step, and for me that was huge. Up until then I'd rarely taken a step of any size toward achieving something I really wanted to do (getting a copywriting job at an ad agency didn't count, since it was just another example of my settling for something safe and practical instead of believing in myself and becoming a *real* writer).

But this time I was giving myself a glimmer of a chance at something: acting. Well, soap opera acting, anyway. I was newly married, working full time as a copywriter by day, and memorizing soap opera scripts by night. The workshop was twice a week from 9 p.m.– 11 p.m. As the weeks wore on I became exhausted. I was moody. I was nauseated. I was bloated. I was pregnant. I figured nobody would want to hire a pregnant girl for a soap opera, and so I stopped going to the workshops. Like so many times before, I told myself "no" before someone else had a chance to. I figured I'd go back to it someday—at least that's what I told everyone. But when?

Eight years later, when my kids were in school, one of their friends' mothers asked me if I'd ever done any acting work. "You have a very commercial look," she said. Turns out she was a partner at a talent agency that specialized in commercials. She told me she'd represent me if I ever decided to give it a go, but I told her "thanks, but no thanks," since I had my hands full with the kids. Here was someone willing to give me a "yes," but I was still giving myself a big fat "no." Looking back now I think I was afraid that if I went for it, I might not have succeeded. But at the time I just used my old trusty excuse of being too busy with my family to give it a shot. And that continued to be my story until I found myself making that list of mine. Acting was something I'd always dreamed of doing. It was, like I said, one of the few things that I'd ever made even the tiniest of steps toward achieving.

Another seven years went by before I made my list, but I hadn't forgotten that dream. And so, I put down "get a paid acting job." The next time I saw that mother of my daughter's friend, I took a deep breath and asked, "Remember say six or seven years ago, when you offered to represent me if I wanted to try doing commercials? Is that offer still good?"

"Go get your head shots done," she said.

At my first audition I was so nervous you'd have thought I was trying out for a role in *Titanic* and not in a toothpaste commercial. But the more I auditioned, the more comfortable I became. I learned what to wear (jeans or khakis, pastel-colored shirt), what not to wear (anything dark, patterned, or too revealing unless the part called for it). I learned that I had to check the board upon arriving at a casting director's office, sign in, bring head shots, résumés attached to the back, fill out a size card if requested, download any sides (pages of a script), and memorize them even though they were often thrown out the window in favor of new dialogue scribbled on cue cards. Then one day it happened. I got called back. I was one step closer to booking a real paid acting job. I didn't get that job, or the next however many I got called back on. But the callbacks did keep coming. Then, out of nowhere, it happened. I got picked.

The job was for DirecTV, which was ironic since I used to have DirecTV and I hated it. Now I was going to be doing a commercial for this fabulous amazing perfect company. And not *just* TV—I'd be doing print, too! I had four wardrobe changes and a fake husband. I had fake friends and fake kids. I even had a fake father-in-law to complete the perfect family portrait. Just like Norman Rockwell would have painted, had Norman Rockwell had DirecTV. Was I a hypocrite for promoting a company that I'd always believed to have substandard service? No! Why? Because I was an actor! A real, honest-to-God working actor! And while I, Susan Campbell Cross, detested and loathed DirecTV, "Blonde Mom" did not. I didn't have to love DirecTV, I just had to play the part of someone who did. And that, my friends, is *acting*.

I realize now that the reason I never managed to shine in my childhood attempts at acting probably had little to do with my acting ability, and a lot to do with my abundance of nerves. I don't think for a minute that if I hadn't written "get a paid acting job" on my list that I would have ever given it a real shot. Somehow seeing it there in black and white reminded me that it was a dream unfulfilled. And while I might get a lot of noes, my own should not be one of them. The only way to make sure that there is no chance of getting a part is to not audition for it in the first place. I'm not saying that I am now completely nerve-free when I go out on calls. It's just that I have decided that my nerves are not insurmountable fear. They are just nerves, and I can work through them.

~~#15 Get a paid acting job~~

· · · ·

I crossed "get a paid acting job"—the last of my performing-themed goals—off of my list. I had a new side gig as a commercial actor, some fun new musical loving friends in the neighborhood, and the ability to play a couple of songs on the guitar. I'd also gained a lot of personal insight. Why was it so easy for me to convince myself I wasn't a good enough actor to go for it as a young adult? And why, when I finally did make a half-hearted attempt at giving my acting dream a chance, had I pulled the plug on it the second I found out I was pregnant? After achieving these goals, the answers to those questions became clear.

When I first started taking on the performing challenges on my list, I was doing so in an effort to get some sort of proof that I was good enough. I was still looking for approval from the outside instead of from within. The further I got into it, though, the more I found a new motivation: I began to perform simply for the joy of it. Without the pressure to impress, I relaxed, and the more I relaxed, the better I got. The better I got, the more confident I became. The more confident I was, the more I enjoyed it. And that's why I continue to do it. I love it when people like what I do, but now, I don't rely on that to feel good about myself. I know I'm doing my best no matter what I take on, whether I'm performing for a live audience, a camera, my children, or the shampoo bottle. In other words the only approval I really need is mine.

When you make your own list, look for common themes among whatever your goals are. Hidden within those themes are secret messages that are all about you. What they are, and what they mean is something only you can figure out. If it takes some time, don't worry. Just keep on living your list and taking on the challenges you set before yourself, and little by little you will start to receive your messages. And the loving, encouraging, positive voice that will deliver them will be your own.

GIRL IN THE 'HOOD

When I tell people what's on my list, I get a wide range of comments that include everything from, "Are you crazy?" to "I would never!" and "You *are* kidding, right?" One that I've heard more than a few times though, is, "How is *that* even a challenge?" I appreciate people's opinions, I do. But, the best thing about my list is that it's mine. It doesn't have to make sense to anybody else. I get to decide what's important to me, what isn't, and what the criteria is for something to be worthy of a spot on my list.

It is true that some of the things on my list were easier to pull off than others. Some required serious soul searching, and some just had to do with my desire to experience something, complete something, or be a part of something. While not everything on my list resulted in life-altering revelations. I believe firmly that every challenge I took on was worthwhile and provided me an opportunity to grow, both in wisdom and in experience. When you make your list, you can come up with your own goals and base what makes them list-worthy on whatever you want. If they aren't all the same level of difficulty, so be it. A few of the challenges on my list were less difficult in part because they could be achieved right in my own neighborhood. Some of them were even specific to my neighborhood and to my neighbors. I wrote on my list the following challenges: "get to know the neighbors," "start a neighborhood tradition," "ride my bike," and "play bitch's bingo." Clearly, these were not the most difficult goals, but I had my reasons why I wanted to achieve them. And, like a lot of the other challenges on my list, these reasons stemmed from my childhood.

I live in a suburb of Los Angeles, tucked away north of the 101 Freeway in the San Fernando Valley. I love living here in large part because it feels a lot like where I grew up, but with nicer weather. In Pittsburgh I'd lived in a neighborhood called Squirrel Hill. The residents of Squirrel Hill knew their neighbors beyond the occasional, "May I borrow a cup of sugar?" sense. We had real relationships with the people who lived around us. My dad and stepmother still live in the same house they bought when they got married, and their neighbors are like extended family: they take trips together, have book clubs, and do covered-dish parties. These are the folks who count on each other to bring by chicken soup when someone has a cold and to bring in the mail and feed the cat when someone goes out of town. They attend one another's big family events: baptisms, bar mitzvahs, and weddings, as well as funerals, shivas, and wakes.

I've been fortunate to have friendly neighbors in all of the neighborhoods I've lived in since moving to California but, hands down, Hidden Hills has been the closest thing to what I experienced growing up. When we moved to Hidden Hills, I was blown away by how welcoming the neighbors were on our little cul-de-sac of a street. It wasn't even a street, really, more a private driveway. Sounds fancy, but it's only called that because it's not wide enough to be considered a real street. As a result of the narrowness of our private driveway, the five houses on it are very close together. At first I was concerned about this; if we hadn't gotten along with our new neighbors, it would have been really uncomfortable. Within a few minutes of living there, though, I knew we were going to be just fine.

While our moving truck was being unloaded, twin boys came over to ask if we had any kids. They lived in the house on the end and were one year older than Kayla, who was ten at the time. Their mother, also named Susan, stopped by with a plate of chocolate chip cookies. I liked her immediately. She looked around at the 8 million half-unpacked boxes. "You could use a margarita." She said, stating the obvious.

I laughed, "Yeah, well, as you can see, I have no idea where my blender is!"

"I know where mine is," and God bless her, she went back to her place and returned with two giant margaritas. Cookies and cocktails, I knew I was home. I couldn't imagine that all our new neighbors were going to be as nice as this one, but they all were. Norma and Neil Diamond (but not *that* Neil Diamond), an older, retired couple lived at the end of the drive, right next door to us. Their kids had grown up and moved away, and now they were happily pursuing their passions: he tended to his horses, and she painted in oils and watercolors.

The neighbors directly across were Tracey and Shaun Cassidy. Unlike Neil Diamond, he actually was *that* Shaun Cassidy. While I don't remember this *at all*, my dad insists that I had a huge crush on Shaun Cassidy when I was eight years old and that I carried a lunch box with his face on it and played *Da Do Ron Ron* over and over on the record player. I was nervous to meet them. I wondered if they were going to be regular people like we were, or if they were going to be the pretentious, "I'm too famous to bother talking to you" type. The moment of truth arrived when Tracey, who was very, very pregnant at the time, came over and introduced herself. I was out front with the kids. Aidan, who was five, took one look at her and said, "I'll bet you're having a baby!"

"That's right," she laughed.

"You want to know how I know?" Aidan asked, and before she could answer he burst out, "Because you are soooooo fat!" I was mortified. I wished at that moment the ground would open up beneath me and swallow me. Tracey just laughed and laughed and any fears I had about not being able to relate to our neighbors went right out the window.

The Biernats were next door to us on our left and were just as nice as all the others. They had four kids, all but one off to college already when we moved in. We saw all of our neighbors on our little street frequently, in part because the houses were so close there was no way *not* to see them. But we also got together for meals and trips to Costco, holiday parties, and barbeques. It felt a lot like Squirrel Hill. Unfortunately, it also felt a bit cramped.

We had moved from a larger house to this one, and while we loved the openness of the downstairs floor plan, the bedrooms upstairs were tiny, especially the kids'. There was barely room for a bed and a nightstand. They each had a built-in desk on one wall and a small dresser and shelves in their closets, and that seemed like all they would need when we bought the house. After all, they were little kids. But the thing with little kids is they get bigger. And their clothes and shoes get bigger, too. Their rooms, however, stayed the same size. They spent almost all their time downstairs in the kitchen/family room, which was also where I spent most of my time. There was a lot of togetherness, especially when they had friends over. Which was pretty much all the time.

After we'd been cozy (and by cozy I mean cramped) there for three years, I started to wonder if there might be a house we could afford that still was in Hidden Hills but with larger bedrooms and better storage. I made a call to a realtor friend and lo and behold, she took me to see two of them when Kevin was out of town. The second house, to quote Goldilocks, "was just right."

It was in the newer section of Hidden Hills, where the houses were farther apart and the streets were wider. I far preferred the older section, with its mature pepper trees shading horses in their corrals. All the houses in Hidden Hills are equestrian properties, but if the people in the newer section had horses, they mostly kept them someplace else or tucked away at the very back of their properties. I didn't want to own a horse, even though I'd managed to work through my fear of riding them thanks to my trusty list. Still, I liked being able to take a walk with a bag full of carrots and apple slices to dole out to the horses that came ambling up to the three-rail fences. There would be none of that in the newer section.

Despite my preference for the older 'hood, I was excited about the house; it had everything I was looking for. It was one-story, with the master bedroom on one side, the kids' rooms on the other, and the common areas in between: living room, dining room, kitchen, den, and an *art studio*. That was something I didn't know I wanted until I saw it. Our middle son is quite an artist, and I could picture him painting away happily in that room, which had wall-to-wall built-ins designed to house art supplies. There was a desk as well that would be perfect for homework, and an entertainment center big enough to hold all their movies and video games. This was going to be the perfect spot for all the neighborhood kids to hang out in on the weekends. I would be the coolest mom on the block.

It didn't take a whole lot of convincing to get Kevin on board and soon the house was ours. Back on our old street, the neighbors were surprised with the news of our move, but they were happy for us. We promised we'd get together often; we were, after all, only moving a couple of miles away. I also looked forward to getting to know the neighbors at our new house. This last part, however, was not to be:

we moved, and within a week or two of living there I realized things weren't like our old street: there would be no cookies and margaritas. I'd assumed that all the neighbors on all the streets in Hidden Hills were just like the ones we had at our last house. I don't know if it's the fact that it took more steps to get from one house to the next or if the neighbors here are all in the witness protection program, but the only time I saw anyone, it was in passing as they'd zip by in their cars and *poof*, disappear into their attached garages and their own lives.

I missed my old neighbors. We didn't end up seeing each other nearly as much as we'd promised we would; those two miles that separated us might as well have been two hundred. I know I'm the one who moved and that I should've been the one to make the effort to maintain the friendships, but you know how that goes. The kids were better about this, though, and they continued to hang out with their pals from our old neck of the woods. But they did it at their houses. That wonderful multipurpose room mostly sat empty on weekends. And I was not nearly as cool as I thought I would be.

I started to rethink our decision to move. Was a little more space worth giving up having close relationships with our neighbors? This was one of the things I was thinking about as I worked on my list. I wanted to reconnect with our old neighbors and make friends with the new. Sure, sightings of the new ones were few and far between, but, as the saying goes, "If Mohammed won't come to the mountain, the mountain must come to Mohammed." I decided to make like a mountain and added, "get to know my neighbors" to my list, followed by, "start a neighborhood tradition." I had an idea of how to accomplish both: I'd have a party.

I always tell the kids that if they want to get more invitations from friends, they have to extend more invitations to friends themselves. When people make guest lists, they think about who invited them to do things in the past. I really needed to start following my own advice. Deciding to do something, however, and actually doing it are two different things. I hate to admit it, but it took a couple of years before I finally had that party. If it hadn't been for a few of my close girlfriends, I still might not have.

We were out celebrating one of their birthdays. The holiday season was in full tilt, and we were talking about a huge party that one Hidden Hills couple throws every year and how this year some of us were not invited. I was one of those. I didn't take it personally; I'd only ever been invited to it once, and that was because I'd had a couple of drinks, marched right up to the husband and asked him point blank, "What do I need to do to get invited to your holiday party?" I guess my pushiness paid off, because I was invited the following December. But the next year, I wasn't. Another of my friends had been invited four years straight but also had failed to make the list this time.

We consoled each other and talked about how great it would be if there was another annual neighborhood party. Not one that would compete with the other one (in case we somehow managed to get back on the guest list next year), but one that would also be fancy and festive and that could also become an annual event that Hidden Hills neighbors could look forward to. The only way to guarantee being invited to it would be to throw it, and, since not one of us had any plans for New Year's, it was a natural decision. We would have a New Year's Eve party, and it would be at my house. Voilà, I not only had plans for New Year's Eve, I finally had plans to accomplish two goals from my list as well.

The first annual New Year's Eve Party at Chez Cross went off without a hitch. I sent out online invitations, saving time on hand addressing and money on stamps. In order to invite some of the neighbors I didn't know, I asked those I did know to send me e-mail addresses of anyone they thought I should include. Because New Year's Eve was only a couple of weeks away, I figured I wouldn't

have the biggest turnout in the world. I think I might have had more
new neighbors in attendance if I'd printed the invitations and put
them in each mailbox with a handwritten note saying something
like, "Hi. You don't know me, but I live on your street. If you don't
have plans for New Year's Eve, please drop by for a champagne
toast." Regardless, we did end up with a crowd of forty-five or so
rabble-rousers, most of whom were neighbors whom I already knew.
Still, there were a few there who I hadn't met before, and I hope that
next year, given that I will send invitations out sooner, even more
new friends will join us.

My plan wasn't as successful as I'd hoped, but that doesn't mean
I'm done trying. If anything, it made me realize that building new
friendships takes concerted and consistent effort. So I crossed "get to
know my neighbors" and "start a neighborhood tradition" off of my
list, and added to my list of New Year's resolutions, "*continue* getting
to know the neighbors," and "start planning the 2nd Annual New
Year's New Eve Party at Chez Cross earlier."

#16 Get to know my neighbors
#17 Start a neighborhood tradition

. . . .

If I learned anything from those first two neighborhood challenges,
it was that wanting something to happen doesn't mean it will. I have
to make a plan and put it into motion, and then, if that plan doesn't
turn out as expected, I have to reevaluate and keep on making new
plans that get me closer to achieving my goal. The key to a successful
plan is action, because without action the plan just stays a plan, and
the goal just stays a goal.

When I set out to "ride my bike," I was looking to put into action
a plan I'd made quite a while back when I plunked down a bunch of
money at the Spoke 'n Wheel bike shop. That fell under the "If you

build it, they will come" philosophy—I actually thought that by purchasing bikes for every member of my family, we would ride them. Just as with my desire to get to know my neighbors, this goal had roots deep in my childhood.

When I was little, parents were not chauffeurs by default. If kids wanted to get somewhere, they had to walk or ride their bikes. I had had a pretty sweet ride back then, a bright-red Huffy with a blue denim seat. That bike was my main mode of transportation, and it was also one of my main modes of recreation. I used to ride around the streets of Squirrel Hill with my friend Margot, who lived across from the cemetery. It sounds pretty creepy now, but back then we didn't give it a second thought. We spent hours on end in that cemetery, collecting snails from the pond and racing up and down the big hills on our bikes. It was our own private racetrack and park. I should take a moment now to formally apologize to any mourners who were interrupted by the whoops and hollers of two little rebels on Huffy bikes between 1979 and 1982.

I stopped riding that bike when I was thirteen after we moved from the little house on Northumberland Street that my mom's girlfriend owned and into a town house on Forbes Avenue. That girlfriend had become an ex-girlfriend. She didn't come with us, and neither did my bike, although one had nothing to do with the other. I am sure that my bike not coming was more a matter of our not having space to store it, and that I'd outgrown it. Until the day we went as a family to the Spoke 'n Wheel bike shop, I hadn't owned another bike, or even been on one.

They say that you never forget how to ride a bike, but I wasn't too sure that was true. My bike, the one I'd bought with the very best of intentions, the one I'd planned to spend hours riding, was still in my garage exactly where I'd parked it the day I bought it. I had imagined our whole family out together, tooling around the neighborhood on our bikes every weekend, but it had never happened. The kids had been very happy to buy the bikes and all the accessories for the bikes, but they didn't really seem interested in riding the bikes. And since they weren't riding theirs, I didn't ride mine either.

Every time I went into the garage and saw the row of bikes lined up collecting dust and serving as housing for countless spiders, I felt a tinge of buyer's remorse. And so I put "ride my bike" on my list. It would be an easy goal to achieve, I figured, because all I had to do was dust it off, put air in the tires, get on, and ride. Only thing, though, was that it had gears. My old Huffy did not.

I was going to have to learn how to ride a bike all over again. My husband had taught me how to drive a stick shift, and so I figured teaching me how to shift gears on my bike would be a piece of cake for him. My kids, sensing that watching me do so would be free entertainment, decided to join us for the ride. I was thrilled that we finally would be riding around Hidden Hills on bikes together as a family. My wish was coming true after all. I was sure that it would be easy for me to get the hang of the gear shifting thing, and that we'd be having fun in no time. But I was wrong.

After a quick lesson and reassurance from my husband, I pedaled off. At first I was okay, maybe a bit wobbly, but still okay. Then it came time to shift gears. That's when the trouble started. I couldn't figure out which lever to squeeze, the left or the right, and did I have to be pedaling during the shift? What if I was coasting and tried to shift? What would happen then? And come to think of it, wasn't one of those lever thingies a brake? All I had to do to stop on my Huffy was pedal backward.

With all my concern over the gears and the brakes, I forgot entirely about the chain, and my pants got stuck in it. I jerked to a stop and had to wait there, straddling my bike, completely embarrassed, while my husband worked at getting the fabric unstuck from the greasy metal trap. I don't remember that ever happening on my Huffy. Once I was free, I rolled my pants up to my knees and tried again. I pedaled and pedaled and then attempted to shift gears. Every time I did, the bike jerked and made some awful scraping noises, and then suddenly, pumping the pedals had little effect. Then I'd shift again and lurch forward as the pedals became nearly impossible to push. All of this was really wearing out my thighs, not to mention my poor butt. I think the denim seat on my Huffy must have been very well padded. This new bike's seat was hard as a rock.

I'd had enough. I'd achieved my goal. I'd ridden my bike. I'd only ridden it about two blocks, but I had ridden it. I pedaled back to our house and put my bike away in the garage. I haven't gone riding since that inaugural run. The kids have, however, and it's great for them. As for me, I believe my best bike riding days are behind me. And that's okay. Not everything on my list was going to become my new life's passion. The important thing was that I set out to do something, and I did it. The list had given me the motivation I'd been lacking to put my bike-riding plan into action. The fact that it wasn't my new favorite form of exercise was of little consequence.

#18 ~~Ride my bike~~

. . . .

Clearly I wasn't destined to become a biker chick and join those spandex clad enthusiasts who rule the trails of Hidden Hills. But there was a group in the neighborhood that I had set my sights on becoming a part of. These weren't ladies who lunch. They were bitches who bingo. And I wanted in.

For women in the suburbs, just as it is for wolves in the wild, there are ways to know when you've been accepted into the pack. It's different for men, they just have to show up once in a while at community functions and mutter something about sports or stocks and they're in like Flynn. It's a much more delicate and complicated process for the women. There's the sizing up period where the new potential member must avoid making eye contact and pretend not to notice as the other females look her up and down and comment to one another in whispers about what she's wearing, where her kids go to school, and whether or not her boobs are her own. If everything meets with the approval of the pack, a scout is sent over to initialize contact.

After that scout has made her report, and only if it's favorable, then the newcomer might be invited to participate in a ritual practiced in suburban neighborhoods throughout our great nation. I'm talking, of course, about bingo. Not just any bingo, Bitch's Bingo. I had lived in Hidden Hills about a year before I made that list of mine, and it had been a year without bingo. The women who play bingo are a fairly big group, not to be confused with the group who plays bunko. They're pretty exclusive, though, and I hadn't managed to earn an invite from that camp.

The bingo gals are a fantastic assortment of women, and I wanted in, so I made it a goal on my list. I knew some of them already and opted to keep on dropping hints until somebody invited me. Finally, when it was one of their turns to be the hostess, I got my very first invitation. Bitch's Bingo is a cutthroat version of the classic church lady game: everybody contributes ten dollars to the pot and brings a wrapped gift valued at twenty-five dollars that goes onto a big table. Each player takes two bingo cards and some Post-its, so they can label the gifts they choose and unwrap each time they win a game. Once all the gifts are claimed they go back on the table, so that during the next round, people can steal them. That's where the bitch part comes in. If you win during that round, you get to pick what you want and replace the original winner's Post-it with your own.

Sounds harmless enough, right? Add some wine and see what happens. Actually, for the most part everyone plays nice and nobody gets their panties in a bunch if they don't end up with the prize they wanted, or any prize at all, which does happen. Some people don't get a bingo during the second round, and some people, like me, get more than one. Before you think I'm lucky, let me tell you what happened to me at my first-ever Bitch's Bingo party.

Every time I got bingo, I got shot the evil eye from a tall blonde a couple of tables over. As I passed by she said, "You better not steal anything with my name on it, or any of my friends' names on it either." This got her friends laughing, and me sweating. Just great, I thought. I had already managed to piss off the women I was hoping to make friends with. Nervous, I looked at the booty on the table. I didn't know all the names of the ladies yet, and so it was hit or miss as to whether I would, indeed, steal something from one of the mean girls. To my misfortune, my luck held all night. I managed to walk out of there with four gifts, at least three of which had been previously claimed by one of the women at the mean table. The round ended, blackout bingo was played, and the person who marked all the squares on their card won the cash pot. Thankfully, that person wasn't me.

The next day I told my friend the hostess about what had happened. She knew exactly whom I was talking about. "She's a big pussy cat!" she laughed. "You just need to get to know her better, that's all." But every time I ran into that pussy cat around the neighborhood, my heart started racing and I felt my flight instinct kick in. Over the next few months though, I realized that she always waved at me with a smile—not a torch or pitchfork.

I asked a couple of other women in the neighborhood about her, and they all said the same thing: she is a sweetheart. She might be a little rough around the edges, but that's just her sense of humor. You'll see. And over time, I did see. I got to know her at various neighborhood events, including Bitch's Bingo, since I was now on the e-mail list, and I saw that they were right.

It felt, in a way, like I'd been invited to sit at the cool kids' table in the cafeteria. It was nice to partake in a neighborhood tradition, and in doing so I managed to break into the pack, learn a new game, win some awesome tchotchkes, and make some new friends. If you have anything like Bitch's Bingo in your neighborhood, I highly recommend you give it a try. And if you don't, why not start a group of your own? It's an easy way to make friends, as well as an excuse to have a night off once a month or so.

~~#19 Play Bitch's Bingo~~

. . . .

If a goal on your list seems too easy to count as a challenge, don't worry. If it came to mind when you asked yourself what you really, truly wanted to do, then it's just as significant as any other goal. Don't look at the fact that it's easier physically or emotionally to achieve as anything but a positive. In fact, I think it's great to start off your journey with a few of these types of goals. Conquering them won't take long, and you'll gain some of the confidence and momentum you'll need to take on more challenging goals. Peppering these lighter ones in between the more difficult activities will help you to stay balanced and motivated throughout the process. Just because something is easier to achieve doesn't mean it's not important. The two aren't mutually exclusive.

GOOD GIRL GONE BAD

would never describe myself as a prude. Still, there were a few things of a risqué nature I had never done that most people have done by the time they hit midlife. I know this because I asked around. My friends were surprised to learn that I hadn't done these things, and most of them didn't see what the big deal was. Even *I* wasn't clear on why I'd never done them, since I'm such a free spirit and not at all prudish. I looked back on my life and tried to recall whether there were opportunities to do some of the bad-girl type activities that I'd missed, or if I'd simply avoided them. Not that I'm a prude, because I most definitely am not. And since I'm not, I was convinced that it would not be remotely difficult for me to accomplish these next challenges. I was sure there was a bad girl inside me somewhere, and I was determined to let her out. At least long enough to sunbathe topless, crash a party, go clubbing VIP-style in Vegas, go to a strip club, and go skinny-dipping.

. . . .

When it came to "developing," I was somewhat of a late bloomer and always felt embarrassed to change in the locker room before gym class. It seemed to me that the other girls were part of some special club and I just did not belong. They were buying training bras, and I had nothing to train.

The first time I asked to shave my legs was greeted with a firm, "No." While my mother didn't think there was a point, as what little hair there was on my legs was blond, I felt like somehow in shaving it I would be enticing hair to come out other places, tricking my body into believing it was in puberty. But she was a doctor and knew better.

I, being a twelve-year-old, thought she knew nothing, and while on vacation with my father and stepmother I got my chance to give shaving a try. We were visiting my stepgrandparents in Delaware, and one afternoon, after we'd spent the day at the beach, I was in the bathroom about to take a shower. While I was waiting for the water to warm up, I saw my father's dob kit just sitting there on the vanity, open, and I could see his razor sticking out. And then, as if by magic, it was in my hand.

I put about half a can of his Barbasol shaving cream (yes, that too somehow flew out of the dob kit and into my hands) onto my right leg and set my foot on the shampoo shelf in the shower.

Here I should probably mention that there was a window in the shower that opened out onto a screened back porch. The window was left open so the bathroom wouldn't get steamed up, and it was covered by opaque blinds so that nobody could see in. Of course, I couldn't see out, either, so I was completely unaware when my stepmother came in the back door and onto that porch. I was still standing there on my left leg with my right leg propped up on the shampoo shelf, the razor gripped tightly in my trembling hand poised and ready to make that inaugural stroke. The moment it touched my skin my stepmother yelled out, "JIIIIIMMMMM? Did you rinse your suit out?"

Startled, my hand jerked involuntarily, dragging the razor up my ankle and removing a nice strip of skin. Blood started pouring out immediately and streaked the white tub red as the water washed it down the drain. I stood there not knowing quite what to do. For a second or two I felt nothing, and then the sting of the Barbasol in the open wound kicked in. Hot tears came and I realized that I was not going to be able to hide this. They might not have noticed that my legs were shaved—like I said, the little hair I had was blonde, and I doubted my mother would've informed my father that I wasn't yet allowed to shave. I'd figured if anyone said anything I could just casually respond, "Oh, yeah, sure, I've been shaving my legs for years now, didn't you notice?"

The gash on my ankle, however, was unlikely to go undetected. I quickly rinsed off and stepped out of the shower. The cut was still bleeding profusely and now there was blood on the shampoo shelf, dripping down the tile wall of the shower, streaming down the side of the tub and running toward the drain. I looked down and saw that I was also getting blood on the cotton bath mat, and I wadded it up and tucked it in a corner. By then, the blood was free flowing onto the tile floor, so I grabbed some toilet paper and tried wiping it up, but I went through a whole roll before realizing that the cut was producing blood faster than I could clean it. This was bad. I fished around in the medicine cabinet and came up with some Band-Aids. The blood soaked right through those. I started to cry.

My dad knocked on the bathroom door. "Are you still in there?" He asked.

"Dad?" I sobbed.

"What's going on in there?" He said trying to open the locked door.

"Nothing. Well. I um. I kinda. I got cut." It was most of the truth. I had gotten cut. I just left out the part about how.

"Can you open the door?" He asked sounding worried.

"Don't be mad," I said.

I clutched a bloodstained towel around my body with one hand and unlocked the door with the other.

"Jesus Christ!" He said when he saw all the blood. It looked like the shower scene in *Psycho* after Anthony Perkins was through with Janet Leigh. "What the hell did you do?"

"I borrowed your razor," I said.

"You should have asked me first. My razor is very sharp." As if I hadn't figured that one out the hard way.

He folded up a washcloth and told me to apply pressure while he swiped at the blood on the floor and in the shower with the already stained bath mat. "A little bleach and it'll be good as new," he said. Maybe the bath mat would be, but what about my ankle?

It finally stopped bleeding and scabbed over. But my little incident left a permanent scar. It would be quite a while before I attempted to shave my legs again; good thing I really didn't need to in the first place. Eventually my mom relented and gave me a Lady Schick electric shaver. Over the next year or two I caught up with the other girls physically. But I still changed in the bathroom stall instead of out in the open locker room.

. . . .

That early modesty stayed with me through my adolescence and right into adulthood. This is probably why I'd never been skinny-dipping, or mooning, or flashed my boobs while driving on the highway with a group of crazy friends. Nope. Not me. I kept completely buttoned up when in the company of strangers. As I was making my list I realized that this was a decision not based on any moral resignation, and certainly not based on any religious practices, but rather on fear. Yes, on some level I still was that prepubescent girl hiding in the bathroom stall, fearful of someone seeing me and laughing (which never actually did happen, for crying out loud), feeling ashamed of my body, as if it weren't "normal." But you know what? It *is* normal, damn it! In fact, it's *better* than normal: it's pretty darn good, if I do say so myself. I work out. I eat right. I get whistled at sometimes when I walk past construction sites. What was I afraid of? I decided that should the opportunity arise, and if it made sense to do so, I might take the top down.

My big chance came when my husband and I took a trip to Miami and stayed at a boutique hotel, a trendy place right on the beach. This was the kind of place families steer clear of because the restaurants serve eclectic foods (as in no chicken nuggets), there's a big club scene every night, and a rather large number of foreigners stay there. That means that the beach, while not officially topless, is topless nonetheless. I found this out as we headed onto the white sand to set up our beach towels and take in a little sun. I looked to my right and there was a woman with a very cute bikini bottom on, and no top. She was joined by a friend who was wearing a darling oversize, floppy straw hat, cute bottoms, and, you guessed it, no top. I tried to look the other way, but when I did I saw yet another woman with no top. It seemed that I was the only woman there who was wearing both pieces of her two-piece. I started thinking. What would happen if I ditched my top? I might really enjoy feeling the sun on my skin. Skin that had, up until now, never seen the light of day let alone the warm Florida sunshine. Tempting.

I wondered what my husband would think if I went all *European* on him all of a sudden. I shot him a quick glance and saw that he was trying not to get caught taking in the view—the view of all those *other* women's boobs. In one smooth motion I pulled the string and that was that. I shoved my bikini top into my beach bag and settled back down on my towel. Why not, I thought. When in

Rome . . . er . . . when in South Beach . . . whatever. I was already topless.

I looked over at my husband. Now he was definitely looking at me. He was looking at me with a face that read both surprised and pleased. He didn't say a word. Not a peep. Not even when the cabana boy came by to see if we wanted lounge chairs. Or a few minutes later when he returned to see if we wanted an umbrella. Not even when he stopped back by to see if we'd like drinks. Or lunch. That beach has the most attentive cabana boys in the world. Or maybe this is true at all beaches where the women are topless. No matter, I was feeling fine. Liberated.

Yes, it was all going great for me *and* my boobs until, I heard a little boy say rather loudly, "Mooooom! That lady isn't wearing a shirt!" Uh oh. When had they arrived?

"Shhhhh," the mom hushed her son. She was wearing a one piece, a *very conservative* one piece.

"But Mooooommmm!!!" the boy shouted persistently, "*WHY* is she not wearing a shirt?"

"Shush now, it's okay," she said arranging his sand toys so he'd be facing away from my nakedness, "Some people in other parts of the world don't wear the top part of their bathing suits at the beach. It's okay."

"NO IT ISN'T!!!!!" He shouted. He was clearly upset by the notion that women could do that, were doing that, in fact. Myself included.

I had already rolled over in an effort to cover up. The other women were ignoring the kid and still enjoying the sunshine. I was jealous *and* worried. How was I going to get that top back on without showing the girls again? The kid was clearly traumatized. I tried reaching into my beach bag while still keeping my chest firmly pressed into my towel. I fished around in search of the other half of my bikini and came up with . . . a tank top. That'll work! And I somehow managed to get it over my head and my boobs in a swift motion that would have made even the best of magicians scratch their heads in wonderment.

"I think I've had enough sun," I said and started shaking out my towel.

"Really?" My husband seemed disappointed to be leaving so soon. Unlike that kid, he was the opposite of traumatized. Whatever that is.

"Yes. Really." My modesty and embarrassment had come flooding back the second that kid pointed out my nudity. And as much as his mother was right about there being women in other parts of the world who go topless at the beach, I was not one of them. And we were not in another part of the world. And on this particular American beach, regardless of whether people "looked the other way" (at least figuratively), it was still illegal. That was enough sunshine for the girls. They were looking a tad pink anyway. That doesn't mean I won't do it again! But maybe next time I'll wait until we're actually in one of those other parts of the world.

#20 ~~Sunbathe topless~~

· · · ·

In the end, sunbathing topless was less of a hang-up for me than I'd expected. Aside from my boobs, two other things were exposed, namely that I don't like breaking rules and I don't like being caught. Another of my "bad girl" challenges was going to put me at risk of doing both. I had to crash a party.

There had been plenty of times when I'd heard about a party I hadn't been invited to, and it always made me feel bad. But in spite of friends urging me to "just go anyway," I could never bring myself to crash. No, I always felt it better to miss out on all the fun, and then complain about it to anyone and everyone who had the misfortune of mentioning the party within earshot, so as not to miss out on any of their sympathy.

In Hidden Hills there are some pretty extravagant parties. Some are formal, some are casual, and some are just straight out wild, especially the ones thrown by a certain couple who used to rent a certain house that is rumored to be haunted. The previous tenant also had wild parties there, one of which got out of hand and apparently resulted in the death of a guest who drowned in the swimming pool. This same pool was still the subject of much gossip because of the many adult swim parties the new tenants threw. When I say adult swim, I am not referring to kids having to get out so grown-ups can swim laps. No, these adult swim sessions involved skinny-dipping, partner swapping, and group exercise (okay, sex). I didn't make up the rumors, I'm only spreading them, and if anyone reading this lives in Hidden Hills, don't even try and pretend you haven't heard them before.

So one autumn this couple was throwing one of their big shindigs, and I knew it was a perfect setup for my challenge. Why? It was a Halloween party, the best kind of party to crash. Everyone would be in costume, so it would be hard to tell who anybody was, let alone whether or not they'd actually been invited. My plan was to just show up, make the rounds, see if there was any evidence of those rumors being true, and hightail it out of there. I went with Kevin and my friend Nancy and her husband Read (who actually had been invited). We arrived late, having spent the first part of our evening at a kinder, gentler Halloween party. By the time we got to the house of (alleged) horrors, the party was in full swing, no pun intended. The host was extremely drunk and dressed appropriately as Jack Sparrow. The hostess was all latex and silicone, and I'm not just talking about her Cat Woman costume. I suppose if there had been anyone at risk of drowning in the pool that night, she could have served as a floatation device.

As it was, most of the action was taking place on dry land, the dance floor. They had a DJ, who at one point called for volunteers for some kind of game he was going to play. The host took the mike and did his best to convince some of the ladies, and only the ladies, to line up for this game. My friend Nancy, always up for a good time, took the bait. She stood there with about five other women while the host began explaining how it was going to work. As if his slurred speech wasn't enough, he also has an accent, so it was hard to make out what he was saying. Something about the DJ and taking off clothes. The next thing I knew, Read jumped up and tried to get to Nancy, but the host stood in his path and told him to just relax. This, of course, only made Read more determined to get his wife out of that line. The music started and the DJ took the microphone back and started coaxing the girls who were still up there to remove an item of clothing—his clothing, not theirs. Either way, it was a bit more than we had bargained for, and so we slowly made our escape.

Crashing this Halloween party was more of a trick than a treat, at least in my opinion. Most everyone else seemed to be having a great time, but I was tired, my feet were killing me, and I was ready to go home. I didn't bother to thank the host and hostess on our way out, but I highly doubt they noticed. They have since moved out of the neighborhood, and out of the country from what I understand, and I think the group that used to party/swing with them disbanded. I haven't caught wind of any rumors to the contrary, anyway.

Party crashing wasn't nearly as much fun as I'd hoped it would be, and I'm not sure I'll do it again. The next time I hear about a party that I wasn't invited to, I'll think hard about whether or not it's the kind of party I'd like to attend in the first place. If it is, maybe I'll go the middle-of-the-road route and try to let it slip to the hosts that I'd heard about the party they're planning and was really hoping for an invitation—if they have space for me that is—and if so, what can I bring?

#21 ~~Crash a party~~

. . . .

Since I was somewhat scandalized by the party I crashed, I decided to dial back the debauchery by going somewhere known for the high moral standards to which it holds all who visit its fair city. I'm talking about Vegas, baby! I had been there many times with my husband, both before we were married and after. But my personal experiences were always considerably tamer than the stories I'd heard from people who failed to let what happened in Vegas stay in Vegas. I was always more of a spectator when it came to wild behavior, even in Sin City. In fact, I'd even written a post on my *Secrets of a Suburban Soccer Mom* blog:

> I recently went on a little getaway with my husband. We wanted to go somewhere quiet, quaint, romantic . . . so where did we go? Vegas, baby.
>
> Las Vegas is aptly nicknamed "Sin City." Visitors board their flights as perfectly respectable, law-abiding, church-going citizens, but once they've landed at McCarran Airport, all bets are off. Who needs restraint and decorum when booze is free and gambling is legal? Yes, it's easy to succumb to the debauchery that abounds in Sin City. But, as I discovered on this trip, it's just as easy to learn a lesson or two.
>
> Usually the only moral people leave Vegas with is, "A fool and his money are soon parted." That and maybe, "Beer before liquor,

never sicker, liquor before beer, never fear." So this trip I decided to play it cool, abstain from any memory-erasing behavior, and take notes. Here's what I came away with—these are words of wisdom—take heed people!

- You only have to bet big to win big. Unfortunately, you only have to bet big to lose big.
- Expensive does not always mean good. It does, however, always mean expensive.
- Sunshine is free. Shade will cost you (to the tune of $500 per day for a poolside cabana).
- Hookers are hard to spot when everyone is dressed like a hooker.
- What barely stays in your too-tight dress when sober, will absolutely, positively not stay in when drunk.
- Dealers and croupiers are not experts at winning. If they were, they would not be dealers and croupiers.
- There is a direct correlation between the amount of money one saves by having lots of free drinks and the amount of money one loses by gambling while intoxicated.
- Bargains don't come cheap. At least not when the cab ride to the outlets costs $40.
- What happens in Vegas does not stay in Vegas. It gets posted on YouTube, Facebook, MySpace, and for all you famous people out there, TMZ.
- If there is anything truly beautiful and wondrous in the world, you will find a cheap replica of it in Las Vegas. Really. They have New York, Paris, the pyramids, the canals of Venice, and now that Madame Tussaud's Wax Museum has opened, Brad Pitt. I don't know what the moral is there, but I'm sure it will come to me, probably while I'm

floating down a fake canal, in a fake gondola, guided by a fake gondolier, with a fake Italian accent.

Don't get the wrong idea—I had an incredible time. I will definitely go back soon. But, I will do so a bit wiser now that I've learned these valuable lessons. Or . . . I could just squeeze into something with a hem up to here, a neckline down to there, order myself a double shot of tequila (on the house, of course), and live a little. Because perhaps the most important lesson of all is: When in Rome, or in this case Caesar's Palace . . . well, you know the rest.

I was serious when I wrote that last part, but I knew that I would never be able to go completely off the reservation if my husband was along for the ride. No, that kind of wantonness had to be reserved for the company of women. I needed support, the opposite of the moral kind. My friends, Kathleen, Lisa, Nancy, and Valerie, joined me on what I hoped would be a wild-and-crazy VIP Vegas-style adventure. To tell the truth, though, I wasn't too sure how wild we were going to get, considering that Kathleen had done most of the organizing of the trip, and she is a kindergarten teacher. On the other hand, in theory, all kindergarten teachers should be fun and spontaneous. How else would they survive being trapped in a room full of five-year-olds all day?

We were soon to find out. A limo driver approached us at baggage claim. He said the person he was supposed to pick up was a no-show, so he was available if we wanted a ride to our hotel. Since he didn't offer us any candy or claim to have lost his puppy, we unanimously agreed to take the ride from the stranger, and piled in. En route to the Mandalay Bay, he made small talk, asking us how long we'd be in town and what our plans were. We told him we were there for one night only, and we intended to hit up the newest, trend-iest, and hardest-to-get-into club of all, the Marquee Club.

It just so happened that this limo driver's friend was head of se-curity at the Marquee Club and so if we needed anything at all, we should let him know. I let him know that what we needed was a way to get into the club. I saw *Knocked Up*, and I had no desire to take part in a reenactment of the scene where Leslie Mann's character is denied entry into a hot club because she was, "Older than shit," as the bouncer put it.

The limo driver made a quick phone call to his pal and passed the phone to Nancy. By the time she was done with him we were on some sort of VIP list and had directions to a VIP entrance to this VIP club. So our VIP weekend was off to a VIP start. That is until we had to wait in a massive line to check into the hotel, only to be told that our suite wasn't ready.

And so, we took our VIP selves to the regular old ladies room, changed into our bathing suits in bathroom stalls, and stored our luggage with the bell captain before heading out to the pool. A couple of margaritas later we were on top of the world again, lounging in the sun and enjoying the attention of a wide variety of would-be male suitors. Waves of men ranging from silent muscle flexers to metrosexual frat boys took turns occupying the space be-tween our feet and the pool. The only man that seemed capable of intelligent conversation was also the only man who appeared to be flying solo, as in no wingmen. While his confidence was attractive, he himself was not. He would come sit by us for 10- or 15-minute stretches and then get up and walk away only to return after the next group of less independent guys had departed (and by departed I mean given up).

There was a mixed group of men and women nearby who actu-ally came over to thank us. Apparently they'd been watching the comings and goings the whole time and appreciated the free entertainment. These keen social observers thought the funniest part was that the silent, muscle-bound guys and the slick, body-hairless frat boy guys appeared to be sincerely offended that we paid more attention to the lone bald and pasty guy, than to them. The fact that four out of five of us were married and wearing rings to prove it was no deterrent to any of these guys. Maybe they figured we'd be up for some of that, "What happens in Vegas . . ." kind of fun. No such luck (for them). We were, however, ready for some more VIP treatment. And, since our suite was finally available, we went inside for some serious glamification.

If Lonny Anderson and Paula Abdul had a baby, she would grow up to look just like my friend Lisa. She is tiny, she is gorgeous, and she would look hot in a hefty bag. When she came up with a plan for us all to wear cheap LBDs (that's Little Black Dresses to those who don't know), I was seriously planning to chicken out, which I think Lisa must have sensed. In a preemptive strike, she brought five or six extra spandex ensembles. There we all were, trying on and trading these scraps of black fabric, lending each other our honest opinions and critical eyes. I'd been concerned about looking too trampy, but in Vegas, there's no such thing. By the time we were all made up and the clouds of hair spray had cleared, I had to admit: we looked hot.

Oh yeah, we rocked those thirty-dollar LBDs. Eat your hearts out Robert Palmer girls. As we made our way through the casino to the taxi queue, we caused some serious whiplash. People even stopped us and asked if they could have their picture taken with us. This may or may not have been because we let it be known that we were the *Real Housewives of Calabasas*. The show does not exist (yet). Regardless, we were definitely getting the VIP treatment from our newfound fans, and lapping it up like champagne and caviar.

We were in high spirits when we arrived at the Cosmopolitan Hotel, home of the Marquee Club. DJ Kaskade was spinning, so it was super-crowded and the line was a mile long. No problem for us, though, since we were VIPs. We went to the entrance as instructed by our limo driver's friend and sure enough, there was a much shorter line being guarded by a very large man in a black suit. He was all business when he asked us who had told us to go there. Thank God I'd written down the man's name. I fumbled through my clutch for the scrap of paper and said, "Glen Hayes." And the giant intimidating-looking man's face broke into a massive smile.

"That's me!" He laughed. "You must be the ladies from the limo!" And he ushered us into the club and to a VIP table right by the main dance floor. We could hardly believe our good fortune. Apparently those tables cost thousands of dollars and are generally reserved by, you guessed it, actual VIPs. The table we were seated at was reserved for the evening, but the VIP who'd reserved it wasn't going to be in until really late. In fact, what's-his-name (who, we found out afterward from our buddy Mr. Hayes, was Reggie Bush!) still hadn't arrived at 2:40 a.m., and after so much dancing, drinking, and people watching, we were too tired to wait around and see whether he'd be open to sharing it with five super-hot middle-aged moms dressed in thirty-dollar black dresses. So, we headed out.

Back at our hotel, we were catching a second wind when we were stopped by a group of guys who were desperately trying to get into the House of Blues. They thought they'd stand a better chance if they were with a group of hot women. Flattery gets you everywhere, including into the House of Blues in the Mandalay Bay Hotel. They thanked us by buying us a few rounds of drinks and allowing us to entertain them with more tall tales about being *The Real Housewives of Calabasas*. Will somebody hurry up and add Calabasas to the *Real Housewives* empire? Because we already have a fan base and are ready to work.

Somehow it got to be 4:30 a.m. and we were still out enjoying our free thank-you cosmos and our fabulous faux fame, just like all good Kardashians and real *Real Housewives* do. It was time to gather the troops and get some beauty sleep. A few hours later we were up and raring to go again, that is until my stomach started lurching. The girls were getting ready for breakfast and more poolside action, and I was stuck on the throne. Even my tummy troubles were VIP appropriate.

I think it was all the vodka I'd put into me, because as soon as it was out of me, I felt like a new woman. We checked out, leaving our bags once again with the bellman, so we could enjoy what was left of our time in Sin City, poolside, rehashing the events of what did turn out to be a very, very VIP experience in Vegas. It was so much fun in fact, that we are planning to do it again, minus the black dresses. This time, we'll be wearing red.

#22 ~~Go clubbing VIP style in Vegas~~

. . . .

There was another of my good-girl-gone-bad challenges that I could have accomplished while in Vegas. That would be, "Go to a strip club." I certainly was with the right group of girls to do it, but still, something stopped me. I told myself that it would be an easy goal to accomplish at home anyway. There must be plenty of strip clubs in L.A. Not every actor can be a waiter, right? But time went by and I still couldn't bring myself to set foot in one. It was the second to last challenge on my list (excluding write a book, which I am doing as I type this), if that's any indication of how reluctant I was to do it.

It may seem odd that I would put "go to a strip club" on my list in the first place. I mean, seriously, even I raised an eyebrow at that one, which is precisely why I decided that yes, it needed to stay on the list. I have never considered myself to be a judgmental person, yet for some reason I had a lot of judgment reserved for strip clubs, the people who work in them, and the people who frequent them. I was raised to think that women are so much more than their bodies and that anyone who objectifies them is an asshole, and the women who allow themselves to be objectified are just sad, weak, poor, ignorant souls who don't have enough self-respect to realize that they could be doing something better with their lives. Not judgmental at all, right? As uncomfortable as I always was about strip clubs, I was even more uncomfortable about my own judgment of them, considering I'd never been inside of one. It was just another thing I had predetermined to be wrong for me, that I associated with being "bad" and that I secretly harbored a deep curiosity about.

As it worked out, I ended up going with my brother-in-law Sean and his wife Marla when I visited New York. They live in Connecticut, but my brother-in-law works in Manhattan. We met at Grand Central Station and the plan was to have a drink there and then maybe dinner. Sean and Marla have three kids, younger than my own, and Sean travels a fair amount for work. Marla hadn't been out for quite a while and was wearing a sexy dress and high-heeled boots, clearly ready for a night of grown-up fun. When the subject of what we were going to do after drinks came up, I jokingly (well, maybe half-jokingly) mentioned that I hadn't yet been to a strip club. Marla immediately sprung into action, asking the paunchy forty-something suits that were at the bar with us where the closest strip club was.

At first they feigned ignorance, but Marla and I were having none of it. Sean looked like he wanted to disappear. "If you want to go to a real strip club of strip clubs, the 'McDonald's of strip clubs' if you will," one suit finally said, "Go to the Hustler Club on Fifty-first." And so we did. On the cab ride over, I started to feel nervous. I had no idea what to expect, and, to be honest, this was the last thing I ever thought I'd do with my brother-in-law and his wife. They are born-again Christians. Not kidding. That being said, I was still the only one of us who'd never been in a strip club.

After Sean paid the twenty-dollar cover charge for the three of us, we checked our coats and entered the main room. It was a lot smaller than I thought it would be, and also a lot cleaner. (At least I think it was clean, it was pretty dark.) There was a tiny stage surrounded by half-moon-shaped club chairs and cocktail tables. This early in the evening there was only a smattering of patrons, so we had no problem getting a table. I would have chosen one farthest from the stage, but my sister-in-law grabbed a seat front and center. I sat across from her, and my brother-in-law sat between us. The rest of the night we told everyone that we were polygamists, and that we had come to the club to shop for wife number three.

There was a girl on stage, slowly swaying to the music. She was topless, wearing impossibly high-heeled shoes, and teeny-tiny g-string panties that completely exposed her enviably cellulite-free ass. I wondered what kind of exercise she did to maintain her figure. My question was answered when she grabbed a hold of the spinning gold pole in the middle of the stage and began performing tricks that rivaled those of the best performers from Cirque du Soleil.

To say I felt uncomfortable would be an understatement. Looking at her seemed wrong, but not looking at her seemed . . . well . . . rude. She was performing after all. Still, I couldn't keep my eyes focused on what she was doing. I was distracted by the basketball game that was showing on two wide-screen monitors on either side of the stage. The cocktail waitress came over, and I ordered a vodka gimlet that I knocked back in three gulps. The liquid courage came in very handy, since my brother-in-law had decided to buy me a lap dance.

I tried to say no, but it was too late. A girl came over dressed only in heels and a g-string and basically straddled me on my half-moon-shaped chair. She was putting her naked boobs in my face and I was making small talk, trying hard to keep my head turned to the side and my eyes on anything but her nakedness. She seemed amused by my discomfort, and she told me to relax and enjoy it. Enjoy it? How? By the time it was over I knew her name, that she had a ten-month-old son, and that she smelled like vanilla body spray. She knew everything about me except my blood type. "She's a chatty one!" she told my brother-in-law, who paid her and laughed. At least someone enjoyed it.

My sister-in-law had made friends with the bouncer when we first came in, and he sent a dancer over to give her a lap dance on the house. This dancer was a lot more aggressive than the one who'd danced for/on me. At one point she told my sister-in-law, "You're hot, and your husband is hot, too. I'd so fuck the both of you." My sister-in-law played along, narrowing her eyes and making her best sexy face she said, "Awww, I'd so fuck you, too, but I'm a born-again Christian, and Jesus wouldn't like that." That shut her up good and quick.

I thought we'd seen the last of her, but before too long she was back. Apparently a group of guys who'd taken over a table next to ours had bought another lap dance for me. "No thanks," I called over to them, "I already had one."

The girl pushed me back into my chair, leaned in, and whispered, "They didn't buy it for you, they bought it for themselves. They like to watch." Of *course* they did. Great. The girl made sure they got their money's worth. She told me to put out my hands. "Now open them," she said, and pulled them onto her naked boobs. At this point my second vodka had kicked in, and I didn't argue with her. Her boobs felt just like my own, I guess. I honestly don't get why lumps of squishiness are so fascinating to men, but if there's anything they like more than seeing lumps of squishiness, it's seeing another woman's hands on top of those lumps of squishiness.

I noticed the dancer had a lot of tattoos, one of which was writing of some kind. I looked at it as an icebreaker, an excuse to start a conversation with someone whom I was sure I had nothing in common with. Turns out it was a poem she had written herself. Maybe we had more in common than I thought. I wish I could remember how it went because it really was quite lovely. I told her I thought she should keep writing. She seemed to appreciate that I was interested in her tattoos and the fact that she had other talents, besides the obvious ones on display at the Hustler Club. She gave me her real name and told me that it's policy that they all use phony names while they're working. That's why you'll never meet a stripper named Gertrude, Martha, or Ruth, or Susan, for that matter. Actually, you very well might, but you won't know it because she'll tell you her name is Crystal, or Jasmine, or Amber. Interesting, isn't it?

In fact, the whole experience was interesting. Once I relaxed a bit, I enjoyed myself. The girls were fascinating, albeit for different reasons than the male customers would think. One gal was from Pittsburgh, like me. Another was working there to pay off student loans. She was a pre-med undergrad at Brown, a native Rhode Islander. She wanted to go to medical school at Syracuse or Vanderbilt, but was most likely going to stay at Brown. We chatted about college, balancing academics with social activities, and how competitive it was to get into med school. I told her my daughter was going to be going to college in the fall, and she also wanted to be a doctor.

I realized that this stripper was far from my prejudged notion of what she'd be like. She was choosing this job because it had flexible hours, paid more than she could get doing anything else right now, and it allowed her to pay down her student loans so that she could continue her education. It was a means to an end, and clearly it was a conscious decision. She didn't seem remotely lacking in self-confidence, nor did she seem ignorant, downtrodden, degraded, or any of the other adjectives I had been so swift to assign these young women.

The customers weren't what I imagined either. They really were quite tame and well behaved. I heard no whooping or hollering, no whistling, of any kind. I didn't see any hands going places where they shouldn't have been going, save one, but the dancer placed the guy's hand there herself, and I'm sure there was an agreement reached prior to the placement of said hand as to how much she would be compensated. I was curious about how much money these women made in an average night, but I wasn't bold enough to ask. I got the feeling they did pretty well for themselves.

Before I realized it, it had gotten pretty late. The place had become a lot more crowded. More dancers had arrived, more men in dark suits, too. These guys were everywhere, keeping a close eye on the customers; ensuring things didn't get out of hand. I left there feeling like I'd had a fun evening out with my in-laws (who stayed after I'd left, by the way!). I think they were enjoying watching each other have lap dances, and building up some energy that they most likely burned off together when they got home later that night. I could see how that would be an erotic and adventurous date for a secure and committed couple, if both parties were into it, of course.

I am really glad I decided to put "go to a strip club" on my list. It was a relief to let go of some of my hypocrisy—to have my status of nonjudgmental person restored. And I think I was also relieved of a modicum of prudishness, if I must be honest. Yes, I have come to realize that there may have been a tiny part of me that was a little bit prudish after all. But I'm a work in progress, and I'm open to personal growth. I just may include "take a pole-dancing class" on my next list. It did look like great exercise, and I wouldn't mind having a cellulite-free stripper's ass.

#23 ~~Got to a strip club~~

. . . .

Actually, having a cellulite-free stripper's ass would've come in handy for another of my "good girl gone bad" challenges—skinny-dipping.

Go ahead and laugh if you must, but I had never been skinny-dipping. I could tell you that opportunity never arose, but I'd be lying. The truth of the matter is, I did have an opportunity to do it, but I was a big fat chicken.

It was way back when I was seventeen and my boyfriend and I had driven out to the suburbs with another couple to hang out at someone's house. I can't for the life of me remember whose house it was, but the parents were out of town. The four of us were making out. The next thing I knew, the friend of my boyfriend and his date stripped down and jumped in the pool.

Even though my boyfriend and I had been together for almost a year, I felt very self-conscious and didn't want him to see me completely naked. I also didn't want his friend and his friend's date to see me completely naked. They were swimming around, having a blast, and I was just standing there, trying to think up an excuse.

My boyfriend wasn't pressuring me to do anything, but I felt pressured anyway, and I was upset with myself for not being able to let loose and have fun. But I took it out on him. I picked a fight, about what I don't recall. Miracle of miracles, it started to rain and the lovebirds got out of the pool and put their clothes back on. The friend's date told me to wait up, and she got in my boyfriend's car with me. The guys followed in the friend's car.

The rain was coming down hard and the road was slick. Suddenly the car was hydroplaning and I lost control. I pumped the brakes, I turned the wheel the direction the car was heading, which was straight into the woods, but nothing worked. We crashed into some trees and finally came to a stop. It was the scariest thing that had ever happened to me, and it's possible that I may have attached a little of that emotion to the concept of skinny-dipping.

Either way, I'd made it to middle age without ever stripping down and jumping into a pool, lake, ocean, or any other outdoor body of water. That's all I thought skinny-dipping was, but after telling my friends I'd added it to my list, I got various different takes on it.

Some said, "You've never gone skinny-dipping? Why don't you just wait until it's dark and jump in your own pool?" Other people told me that if I did that, it wouldn't count. To them skinny-dipping had to be done somewhere you weren't supposed to be doing it. According to them, if I swam naked in a neighbor's pool I'd be skinny-dipping, but if I swam naked in my own pool, well, I'd just be swimming naked in my pool. There had to be a risk factor, the risk being that I could be caught. Some well-intentioned friends, all male, even offered to let me skinny-dip in their pools, but somehow that seemed creepy. Sorry guys. You get an A for effort though. Several of my female friends said that if I did it alone, it wasn't really skinny-dipping. According to them, I had to do it with someone I loved. It seemed that there were an awful lot of rules for something that was supposedly liberating.

Time went by, and I accomplished challenge after challenge, but not skinny-dipping. What was I so afraid of? Did I have a phobia of being naked in front of others, or maybe a phobia of being naked outside? Did I even want to do it in the first place? I thought about why I'd put it on my list. All I could come up with was that it was just one more thing that everyone else seemed to have done, but I hadn't. I wanted to experience for myself what everybody else said was an amazing feeling.

At this point on my list (#24), I'd come to realize there really is no getting around a phobia of any kind—documented or imagined— there was only getting through it. I was going to just have to, pardon the pun, dive right in. I resolved to do just that the very next time any sort of opportunity arose.

A few hours after I'd made that resolution, I got my chance. It was a Saturday afternoon and had been raining on and off all day, but it had finally stopped. My husband asked me if I wanted to go out to lunch with him and the boys, but I decided to take advantage of the break in the rain and go for a quick jog. It had only been three months since my hamstring reattachment surgery. Knowing the jogging was going to leave me a bit sore, I fired up the Jacuzzi before heading out. While I was jogging I realized that Kevin and the boys would be out, and Kayla had been lounging in her PJ's in her room watching TV when I left. She said she was in a lazy mood and just planned to stay in bed all day.

I picked up the pace in excitement. I was finally going to, as they say, git 'er done. When I arrived back home I noticed my husband's car was still gone. I went quickly through the back gate and into the master bedroom through the patio door, stripped off my sweaty workout clothes, wrapped a robe around me, and grabbed a towel on the way back out. The Jacuzzi had been bubbling away while I'd been jogging, and it was the perfect temperature, somewhere between scalding and tolerable. My eyes darted all around the yard. I was alone. The only view into the yard was through the gate to the driveway, and someone would have to be standing pretty close to our driveway to see anything.

I didn't hear any sounds of neighbors, so I figured it was all clear. I nervously slipped out of my robe and into the Jacuzzi. I did it! And man did it ever feel great! I found a jet for my back and got comfortable. I'd brought a water bottle and a book out there. A few pages in and suddenly I heard a door open. Shit.

"Mom?" it was my youngest son. He apparently decided not to go to lunch with my husband and his brother after all. It would've been nice to know this information before I so cavalierly tossed my robe. "What are you doing out here?" he asked, and then he quickly covered his eyes with his hand and turned his back toward me. He was at least a hundred feet from me, and my nakedness was thankfully somewhat blurred by the bubbles of the Jacuzzi. I hope I didn't scar him for life. I seriously don't think he saw more than just enough for it to register that I was nude. Or maybe it was my screaming, "Turn around! Close your eyes! Go back inside!" that clued him in. Regardless, he explained that he was just letting the dogs out to pee, and could I watch them so he could just be on his way. He didn't wait for an answer. Smart boy.

So there I was, just my five dogs and little old naked me. Yes. I have five dogs. I'm crazy, what can I say? They have a ton of energy, and they were excited to see me. They didn't care whether I was nude or not, or whether I was trying to relax or not. They spent the next five minutes or so circling the Jacuzzi and trying to lick my face, which was the only part of me above the water line. Finally they settled down, and so did I. I opened my book again and resumed reading. See? No big deal. Now that Aidan knew not to come out there, I would have some privacy in which to enjoy my skinny-dipping in peace. Or so I thought. A few minutes later, the door opened again. This time it was my daughter, who'd showered and dressed. Clearly she'd changed her plans of lounging and watching reruns of *Law & Order SVU*.

"Mom?" she said, walking across the patio. Then she got a giant smile on her face. "Wait a minute! Are you doing your skinny-dipping challenge?" I nodded, pulling my knees to my chest, trying to cover myself as best as I could. We'd just shared a dressing room at TJ Maxx the day before, so I don't know why I felt the need.

"Right here? Now?" she asked in disbelief. Her tone wasn't judgmental, it was kind of proud actually. She seemed impressed with the fact that I was out there in the middle of the afternoon, naked as a jaybird, just reading a book, like it was no big deal. And you know, it really wasn't. "Well, I'm going over to Emily's," she said, and then she was gone.

I stayed out there for just a few more minutes. I was turning into a prune at that point, and I figured I'd accomplished my goal. I climbed out of the Jacuzzi and quick as lightning, grabbed my towel. I wrapped it around myself, picked up my robe, book, and water bottle and made a beeline for the house. I called out to Aidan, "I'm done! Gonna jump in the shower and rinse off. Can you let the dogs in?"

"Yeah! Okay. In a minute," he sounded annoyed. He hadn't been traumatized after all, he'd simply gone right back to playing video games. While I showered it really started to sink in. I had done it. I had—again, pardon the pun—taken the plunge. But did it truly count? After my shower I dried off and looked up the definition of skinny-dip on dictionary.com.

skin·ny-dip (skn-dp)
 intr.v. skin·ny-dipped, skin·ny-dip·ping, skin·ny-dips *Informal* To swim in the nude.

Well then, there you have it. I wasn't doing, here I go again with another pun, the breaststroke, but I think what I did was definitely skinny-dipping. So, if anybody reading this is one of those people who told me that it only counted if I did it somewhere I wasn't supposed to, let me just ruin your surprise, you're getting a dictionary for Christmas. And for those who said it didn't count if there wasn't risk of being caught, I *did* get caught! Twice! And for those who said I had to share this with someone I loved, I did. I had the company of my five furry loved ones, plus the accidental company of two of my kids. I'd accomplished the last of my "good girl gone bad" challenges. And, like the good girl that I truly am, I met every single requirement everyone had put to me, even though there really are no rules, according to dictionary.com.

#24 ~~Go skinny dipping~~

. . . .

Putting those more risqué challenges on my list was a way for me to step outside my comfort zone. Have you ever played truth or dare? Well this was my way of daring myself to do some things in an effort to find out some truths about myself. For that reason alone every single one of them was worth it. I came to terms with the fact that I did, indeed, have a bit of a prudish side, and then I did something about it. That's not to say that I'm now a regular at the Hustler Club or that I'm planning to join a nudist colony. But, should the mood strike, and I'm in good company, I may just let loose a little more often than I would have previously. Just because I did a few of these "bad girl" things, doesn't mean I'm not a "good girl." It just means I have a sense of curiosity, a sense of adventure, and a little less inhibition than I used to.

When you make your own list, I highly encourage you to play a game of truth or dare yourself. If there's anything that you've ever been curious about but didn't do because it seemed "bad," go ahead and write it down. If it isn't something that could hurt someone else, chances are it won't hurt you, either. It might even do you a world of good.

GOING TO EXTREMES

Some of the challenges on my list may strike you as extreme. I'm not talking about #20 (sunbathe topless), #24 (go skinny-dipping), or even #23 (go to a strip club) from the previous chapter. You've already made it through those ones, and, since you're still reading, I think you're ready to hear about a few adventures that are a completely different kind of extreme—the sporty kind. I've never understood the appeal of extreme sports. In fact, I've spent my entire life trying to avoid extremes of every kind. And as for sports . . . well . . . I never played any. I danced.

Excitement. Adventure. Thrilling. Ballet. One of these words is not like the others. I think you can see where I'm heading with this. Don't get me wrong, I loved ballet, and to me, it *was* exciting and thrilling. But it didn't exactly earn me a reputation as an adrenaline junkie. I had a skateboard and a bike, but back then, who didn't? I was one of those kids who inched her way into the pool instead of doing a cannonball. I just couldn't bring myself to let go.

For some people, being more reserved and cautious is part of who they are. They're wired that way, and there's nothing wrong with that. They are simply being who they are, and they can be happy with themselves for that. The thing is, I was *not* wired that way. And I wasn't happy with myself, either. Inside of me there was a cannon-baller dying to get out. One significant childhood experience (and by experience I mean near-drowning incident) had really affected my ability to "go for it." You'll hear more about that later, I promise! For now, you just need to know that fear kept my adventurous side on a pretty tight lockdown.

When the need to be in control starts to limit what you go after, that's when you have a problem, and man, did I have a problem. Here's what I did when I made my list. I wrote down a few things that at the time felt downright dare-devilish: drive an ATV (all-terrain vehicle), go whitewater rafting, and go zip-lining. Looking at them, even *I* questioned my sanity. What can I say? My inner cannon-baller made me do it. And I am so happy she did.

This wasn't going to be the first time I'd attempted an adrenaline-pumping sport. But it would be the first time I went about it for the right reasons. Way back when I was a teenager I did something rather dangerous, not because I really wanted to, but because I wanted to have friends. Doing something because you want to be liked is not the same as doing something because you'd like to. In fact, doing something because I wanted to be liked led me down a very slippery slope. Literally.

· · · ·

As part of my parents' divorce agreement, my dad did not pay alimony, but he did pay child support. My mother, my sister, and I made do on that and that alone. At that time my mother was a medical student, which didn't really afford her time to work a job on the side. So we three lived on the child support, and my mom took out student loans to pay her tuition. After the divorce we moved into my mother's girlfriend's house, which was in a nice neighborhood. We didn't have money, but most of the kids at my school did and they almost all knew how to ski. I, in typical teenage fashion, wanted to be like everybody else. So, in eighth grade I joined the middle school ski club. God only knows how many chocolate bars I sold in order to afford the annual trip to Seven Springs.

My best friend at the time was one of those kids who went skiing often enough to have her very own skis. I was sporting rentals. Once I figured out how to attach them to my boots, I was ready to go. Where though? I had not signed up for a lesson. "No problem," my best friend said. "I will take you up. You'll get the hang of it in no time. It's super-easy." I decided to change things up and throw caution to the wind—in this case, the hard, cold wind that was tossing us about in our little flying bench on the ski lift. As we ascended the mountain, I could see the rope tow lift below where the sane beginners were slowly and carefully making their way down the slight incline and then grabbing onto the thick rope that would pull them back up the 100 feet that made up the bunny slope. The fact that some of them appeared to be struggling even with this baby run should have told me something. My panic switch, however, seemed to have been disabled by the prospect of skiing like the other kids.

As we approached the top, I started to realize I was going to have to figure out how to get off the damn lift. I scooted my butt to the edge of the seat as I'd seen my friend do, and then as my skis touched the ground and the chair continued on its track I was pushed forward and suddenly, I was skiing. I somehow managed to get out of the way of the next people exiting the lift and side stepped to the top of the slope. When I looked around, however, I didn't see my friend, my *best* friend, the one who took me up there in the first place. Who assured me this was going to be a piece of cake. Only it wasn't. Not for me, anyway. It didn't take long before I figured out she'd started down without me. I tried to convince myself that I could do this. Just point the skis in the direction I wanted to go and I'd go, right? I could just go slowly and carefully down the slope, and then I'd find my friend at the bottom and kill her.

I shuffled my skis to the very edge and pointed them straight down and leaned forward a bit to get going. Man, did I get going. The only thing was, I didn't know how to stop. Or turn. I was starting to pass all the other skiers on what turned out to be an intermediate slope, *advanced* intermediate, to be specific. I was petrified and it showed. Somehow I managed to cross through the trees and onto another, even steeper slope. This one had moguls. I didn't know what they were at that time though, I just knew that now I was not only going Olympic-medal-contender fast, I was popping up into the air and landing hard as if I were a marionette at the mercy of some sadistic puppeteer.

Instinctively, I crouched lower and bent my knees trying to soften my impromptu landings and maintain balance. It worked to that effect, but it also made me go faster. Just then I saw a massive wooden post surrounded by haystacks. It was one of the telephone-pole-size posts that was holding up the ski lift, and I was headed straight for it. I closed my eyes and waited for the worst. But the worst didn't happen. What did happen was that the tips of my skis stuck into one of the bales of hay (probably put there just in case some idiot like me came along), and upon impact my bindings released and my momentum took me right out of my skis. I was lying on my back looking up at the white sky while the lift chairs passed overhead, concerned faces peering down at me, looking for signs of life. They weren't getting any. I didn't know whether I was still there or not until I felt the cold spray of snow shower over my face. A ski patrol hockey stopped right near my head. "Didn't you hear me yelling at you to sit down?"

I thought for a second. No, I didn't recall any sound at all except the rush of air passing over my freezing ears. Somehow I'd lost my hat. Other than that I was pretty much okay. Pissed, but okay. Where on earth was that "best friend" of mine? I found her with some other kids drinking hot cocoa at the lodge. "There you are!" she said as if I'd simply wandered off for a moment. "Ready to go again?" Not by a long shot.

Eventually I did go skiing again. I took lessons and stuck to the beginner and, ultimately, the intermediate slopes. I had absolutely no intention of working my way up to the black diamond runs. I never wanted to see another mogul as long as I lived. After that first skiing experience, I avoided extreme sports of all kinds for fear of winding up at the whim of some external force, whether it is snow, gravity, or whitewater. I found the caution that I'd so cavalierly tossed aside on that ski trip and super-glued it to my very core. I was not about to let go again anytime soon. I felt I always had to be in control. But the trouble with that was the struggle to do so kept me from doing things I really wanted to try. I was *not* in control, my fear was. That is, until my list.

Not long after I started making my way down the list, we were planning a family vacation to Banff, Alberta, Canada. The process of doing my challenges had been working miracles on the super glue and I was once again considering throwing my old friend, caution, to the wind. Before the feeling passed I went online and booked our family on a series of adventure tours.

· · · ·

The first activity involved something that most of us do every day, driving. Easy enough, right? Not exactly. We'd be driving not a car but an All-Terrain Vehicle. As in, a no-doors-no-roofs-no-airbags All-Terrain Vehicle. I had trouble enough with a regular old car!

Before we get into that four-wheeling jaunt, however, a little background: let me say right now that I, unlike Rain Man, am *not*, a very good driver. It's not that I'm a terrible driver, either; it's just that I never really felt comfortable behind the wheel. Maybe things would be different if I'd taken driver's ed. To tell the truth I don't know why I didn't.

I never had lessons from my parents, either. My father never drove—good thing, since he is blind in one eye and therefore has no depth perception. My mother was busy. So I learned from my then boyfriend, Marc, who was a year ahead of me (and who probably took driver's ed). He had his own car, and I practiced on it for hours in parking lots and on side streets before I was finally able to drive in traffic.

I managed to get my permit, and when I did I got behind the wheel of my mother's burgundy Honda Accord, anxious to impress her with my fine driving skills. Mom didn't know I'd already been driving with Marc. "Wow! You're a natural," she exclaimed as I drove effortlessly through the cemetery. No, nobody had died. It was my mom's way of making sure I didn't, as a new driver, kill anybody. "In the cemetery," she said, pleased with her novel idea, "Everybody is already dead!" My mother probably thinks to this day that she is an excellent driving teacher (Mom, if you're reading this, I hate to burst your bubble, but I was *not* a natural, and you were *not* a good driving teacher. But I will give you credit for creativity. I mean, come on, who else would have thought of teaching their kid to drive in a cemetery?).

By the time my sixteenth birthday rolled around I knew what all the different lines painted on the road indicated and had memorized the various signs—even the hand signals. I was proficient in parallel parking and was ready for the driving test. In Pennsylvania, when I was a teenager, the driving test was administered at a police station. It consisted of driving the test administrator around a closed course and then waiting for his or her verdict. I was nervous when a heavy-set woman got into the passenger seat of our Honda.

My mother had made one rule about my driving her car: I was never, under any circumstances, to drive any passenger who was not wearing a seatbelt. So I waited for my test lady to make a move toward hers. I just sat there, not sure of how to broach the subject when she finally broke the silence. "You can start the vehicle now," she said. I wished I could, but my mother's words were ringing in my ears. Could this be a test in and of itself, I wondered? Could my mother have put her up to this? Was this some evil plot designed to trick me into breaking her cardinal rule of driving so that I would not be permitted to use her car? How could I be sure?

While I was pondering all of this, the driving test lady was getting annoyed. "Um," I stammered, "Would you mind buckling your seat belt? Please." The lady harrumphed and shifted her girth back and forth in the little Honda's compact seat.

"I will NOT buckle my seat belt. It is NOT a law in the state of Pennsylvania and I am NOT going to wear it." Hmmm. Sounded somewhat canned, that speech. Could this have been rehearsed previously—a script written by my mother for just this occasion? Again, I had no way to be sure. So, I decided that regardless of the law, making my passengers wear their seat belts was the responsible thing to do. So I waited, hoping she'd change her mind. No such luck. "Are you telling me that you won't start this vehicle until I am wearing a seat belt?" she asked incredulously.

"I guess so," I said hopefully.

"Step out of the vehicle then," she ordered. "Test's over."

But I hadn't even started the engine. How could it be over? I watched helpless as the woman scribbled something on my application, her eyebrows knitted together in frustration (with me, I gathered), and her jaw set. I'd blown it, all right. Back inside, my mother was waiting with an excited expression on her face. Clearly this was not a scheme she'd cooked up. "How did it go?" she asked. I reluctantly handed her the paper the tester had given me. On it in big bold letters she'd written, "Failure for noncooperation." It would be two weeks before I was allowed to test again. Apparently this imposed waiting period between attempts at getting a license was mandatory. That was a law. Wearing a seat belt was optional. Go figure.

My driving career was off to a rocky start. First the failed driver's test and then, about a year later, I had the accident on the night I didn't go skinny-dipping. That accident was terrifying, but I wasn't seriously injured. I'd been wearing my seat belt. Yes, I was wearing my life-saving seat belt even when it wasn't a law in the State of Pennsylvania. What *was* a law in the State of Pennsylvania (in addition to the two-week waiting period between tests) was that I wasn't allowed to drive past midnight until I turned eighteen. Again, for the record: no seat belt, no problem. But drive past midnight . . . *that's* against the law. I would've been in trouble on that count, so my quick thinking boyfriend Robbie (Marc and I had already broken up by then—try to keep up if you can), told the responding policemen that he'd been driving when he hadn't even been in the car. That was terribly romantic, since Robbie had a couple of previous accidents and knew that with this one, his insurance would go sky high. Young love.

After that I never felt confident in my driving. Every time I got behind the wheel I imagined that I might have another accident. And I have, actually, once when I was pregnant with my first child, and another just a few years ago when I was on my way to pick the kids up from the school bus stop. Neither time was it my fault, and both times I was wearing my seat belt. That's a law everywhere now, I think. See? I was just ahead of my time.

Driving is as necessary to people living in Los Angeles as breathing or eating. There are days when I spend upward of six hours behind the wheel without ever leaving L.A. County. Everything is sprawling and rarely can you get anywhere without using the freeways. Our freeways suck, by the way; there's nothing free about them. They should be called parkways, like they are in other cities, it would be a far more accurate description. I drive because I have to get from point A to point B.

So there we were in Banff—an amazingly beautiful place dotted with mountains, lakes, streams, and wildlife—about to embark on our ATV adventure. As I mentioned, ATV's don't have doors or roofs, but they do have giant wheels and *gears*. Uh oh. Banff Adventure Tours informed us that kids under sixteen could not drive their own ATV; they would have to be passengers on the backs of ours. The guide took our youngest, which terrified me. I didn't know what kind of driver this guy was and we were supposedly going to be driving on some rough terrain. Our middle child climbed on with my husband, and our oldest got on behind me.

There was a moment there when the guide was going over all of the things we needed to know in order to drive this oversize Tonka truck when I thought about just getting off and leaving. I was the one who wanted to go there in the first place—part of my "going to extremes" mission. But I really wasn't at all sure I was up for this. What if I couldn't remember how to change gears? And even if I did, what if I didn't know when to change them? What if I flipped over? It was one thing to put my own life at risk, but I certainly didn't want to risk my daughter's.

I leaned back and whispered to her, "I think maybe this isn't a good idea. I'm not sure I can drive this thing. It might not be safe."

She would have none of it. "You drive all the time, Mom. You'll be fine," my daughter said. She had confidence in me, even if I didn't.

"Yes, well, this looks really different than my Mom-mobile," I explained. "It has gears. I have to shift gears, Kayla."

"Didn't you say Daddy taught you how to drive stick?" She asked.

"Yes. But this isn't the same. What if I shift at the wrong time and we flip?" I was really looking for an out here. But Kayla was not going to give me one.

"Look Mom, it's not going to be hard. And if you do mess up, so what? You can't flip us. It'd be next to impossible to flip us. Look at the size of the tires on this thing. And besides, if it were really hard they wouldn't just stick people on these and let them drive after a three-minute explanation of how to do it." She did have some valid points. "Plus, I'm not old enough to drive it and I really want to go." Then she gave me the face. That face she makes that is one part determination, one part pleading, and one part sugar. Works every time.

"Okay," I said. "But just remember I am not sure at all that this is a good idea, and I am not promising you that I'll be good at driving this thing." And off we went, up and down over bumpy trails. About a half hour later I realized the strangest thing. Turns out, I *was* good at it. Sure, it took me a little while to get confident with the whole gear-shifting thing, but my daughter, who hadn't yet had a single driving lesson, was able to feel when it was time to change gears. "Now!" she'd say and I'd shift. Pretty soon I was feeling what she was and doing it unprompted. Little by little I increased my speed. My fear of flipping started to dissipate as I realized that each one of those giant tires operated individually, allowing one of them to drive over a rock without effecting what the others were doing. While I did feel a bit like we were on a bucking bronco, I didn't feel like we were in danger of flipping. It was a jostling, bumpy, noisy ride, but in the end, a lot of fun.

Why an ATV? Because sometimes the most beautiful and awe-inspiring wonders in life are not along the beaten path, that's why. It requires some creative maneuvering and courage to find them. But if you can let go and have confidence in yourself, and have faith that you'll be all right, you might see something few others ever get to see. After we'd been driving off road for a while, we came to a place where the trees were too thick for the ATVs. The guide told us to park them, that we were going to take a little hike, and to bring our cameras. After about ten minutes or so I could feel a huge vibration through my entire body. A steady roaring grew louder and louder until finally we came upon what has got to be the most beautiful thing I've seen in nature thus far: Wapta Falls. While it is not very tall, it is about 500 feet wide. The amount of water gushing over the edge is a staggering 67,363,873,351 gallons to us Americans—that's 255 cubic meters to well . . . practically the rest of the entire world. Tell me again why we don't use the metric system? Anyway, no matter how you measure it, it's a whole lot of water—enough to make Wapta the third largest waterfall in Canada, behind Niagara and Virginia Falls. You'd have to see it to believe it, and the best way to get there? ATV.

~~#25 Drive an ATV~~

. . . .

Driving that ATV really gave me a sense of empowerment and control. In my next challenge in Banff, though, I learned to acknowledge that sometimes I have no control at all; in certain situations, it's best to let things happen on their own. Go with the flow, so to speak. That's the perfect way to put it, actually, since I was whitewater rafting for the first time. Talk about letting go of control! There is no controlling a river. That's for sure.

This ride felt like being on a roller coaster with invisible tracks. I didn't know which way our raft would go until we were already going that way. And then, the current would pick up and pull us another way. We went over some rapids, nothing too crazy, but enough to get everyone in the raft soaking wet. My youngest parked himself at the very front of the raft and caught a face full of water every few minutes. And the water was really, really cold. At one point we came to a place where the water was calmer and the raft had slowed down, and the guide said we could jump in and swim. I thought this was crazy until I saw people launching themselves from a bridge above us. To see them jump from those heights into the freezing, clear water below was inspiring. Not inspiring enough to make me want to join them, though.

#26 ~~Go whitewater rafting~~

. . . .

When I made my list I wanted to be sure to include something that involved heights. Now, I wouldn't classify myself as acrophobic; I was never really afraid of heights themselves. What I suffered from was more a fear of falling *from* heights. And so, in what was becoming an increasingly familiar maneuver—throwing caution to the wind—I took a leap of faith. No, I didn't change my mind and decide to fling myself off of a bridge into a river. I decided to glide *over* one on a zip line. If you've never tried it, it involves sitting back into a little seat made of canvas straps that are wrapped around your legs and attaching yourself to a pulley. You then glide along cables that run on an incline, from pole to pole.

That incline, at least in the first run, was not all that steep. It was just enough of an angle to get us going fast enough to reach the platform at the other end. I watched as my kids went across one at a time, all three of them smiling and laughing. This isn't so bad, I thought. I can totally do this. But it turns out that this was just a warm up. There was a series of these runs and each time the cable was set at more of an angle. As the speeds got faster so did my heartbeat. The last one was the longest and the steepest; it crossed over a river that I do not remember the name of. Funny how quickly one forgets minor details when suspended hundreds of feet in the air over a river by little metal clips and faded canvas straps. But while the name of the river escaped me, the majesty of the view did not.

The eye can only take in so much more when it's looking down from above, and the people on the platform below me got smaller and smaller until they all but disappeared. I could see the tippy tops of the giant evergreens and the dappled sunlight and shadows dancing on the blanket of fallen needles below. The winding river gurgled and gushed to its own rhythm and plan, the silt-like mineral deposits suspended in the water casting blue light in the sun, turning the water into liquid turquoise. My eyes were filled with the whole scene at once, without any man-made interference. That view, coupled with the cool Canadian breeze against my skin as I glided smoothly along the zip line, gave me an overwhelming feeling of freedom I'd never even imagined. I wondered if that's how birds feel all the time. That exhilaration, that pure and utter joy, was all that I felt as I sailed through the air to that last landing platform. As the thrill of flying replaced the fear of falling, any last trace of terror was gone.

#27 ~~Go zip-lining~~

. . . .

Ralph Waldo Emerson wrote, "Life is a journey, not a destination." And he was right. But I know now from firsthand experience that how you feel about that journey can be greatly affected by the mode of transportation. Trying something new, stepping outside your comfort zone, learning when to take control, and when to let go of it, can free your mind of fear, leaving room for it to be filled with a joy and awe that you might otherwise have missed. My new definition of going to the extreme is this: Find something—anything at all— that you wanted to do but were afraid to do, and *do it anyway*. That's right, I said it. Throw that caution to the wind. Or, if you aren't comfortable with that, then at least don't super-glue it to yourself. It's perfectly okay to proceed with caution, just as long as you don't stop because of it. Try it, and you might just see the world, and yourself, in a whole new light.

NINE

GET ~~OVER~~ THROUGH IT

Everyone has physical scars, reminders that we took a spill, lost a fight, or had an accident. They're easy to see and easy to explain. Let's just say you tripped and fell into the coffee table and cut your forehead. The doctor cleaned your physical wound, stitched you up, and in no time at all you were good as new, minus the small scar, of course. What about our emotional scars? They're the ones that occur on the inside when something traumatic has happened to us. We can't see them, and we often can't explain them, but believe me, they're there. They affect how we look at the world and how we interact with others.

If left unhealed, these wounds continue to resurface throughout our lives in the form of fears, manifesting as unhealthy behaviors and attitudes—little red flags alerting us to the fact that something was never dealt with somewhere in the past. And until these issues are addressed, new relationships and experiences will be tainted. We can feel that something isn't right, but we don't always know why. Figuring out the "why" is the key to healing the "what."

Right about now you're probably saying, "How did we go from working our way down a list of fun adventures to working through emotional scars?" It's not as big a leap as you might think. When I set out to accomplish some of the goals on my list, I ran into a few old unresolved issues of my own. There had to be a reason why I hadn't tackled these things sooner, right? When I did tackle them, my issues became—well—an *issue*. I thought I could just get over them, but no. I had to go *through* them in order to move forward.

. . . .

This proved to be the case when I decided I wanted to learn to surf. The story doesn't begin with me signing up for a surfing lesson, nor does it begin with how I avoided signing up for a surfing lesson for years and years. It doesn't even begin with my fear of swimming in large bodies of water. It begins with me falling in love with the beach the very first time I set foot on one.

When I was a kid, my family took a vacation to Prince Edward Island. There are photos of me in my yellow-and-orange bathing suit, the one with a giraffe on it, not that you would be able to see that in the photos. In the photos both my bathing suit and I were a blur. I could not sit still. The ocean was too amazing, the sand too warm. I ran all around and declared it, "The biggest sandbox I ever sawed!"

Years later, after my parents' divorce, my dad took my sister and me to visit his Aunt Eleanor in Sarasota, Florida. She was an odd old woman who lived in a little house with a giant orange tree, the source of all those boxes of oranges that arrived every winter.

Aunt Eleanor wore a wig. I found this fascinating. I'd never known anyone who wore her hair like a hat before. After dinner she would take off her hair and put it on a Styrofoam head that sat on her dresser. She would take it off, and then my father would put it on. Every evening he made us laugh doing his very funny "old lady voice" as he became "Granny Fanny Nestle-Road," a character that he made up strictly for our entertainment.

Florida was an adventure, and to young me, the best part of that adventure was our days at the beach. I'd had several summers of swimming lessons since that trip to Prince Edward Island, but I had yet to try out my swimming skills in the ocean. Now I had my chance. Feeling brave, I followed my sister Elizabeth out past where the waves were breaking into calmer, deeper waters. While we happily swam around pretending to be mermaids, the tide suddenly began to change. The lifeguards were waving and shouting for people to get out; it was too rough to swim. I didn't hear a thing. Elizabeth and I had drifted past the little flags that marked where swimming was allowed.

We were too far to see the lifeguards, and they were too far to see us. My father is a very fair-skinned redhead, so he'd left us to our fun in the water, walking back from the shore to stand in the shade under an awning. He was already pretty badly sunburned due to his Scottish heritage. Not only are Scottish people fair, they're stubborn. And apparently they don't believe in sunscreen. At least my father didn't seem to. So by day three or four of our trip he was dressed in long pants and a long sleeved shirt, his attempt to slow the sun's evil plot to cook him alive. While he was standing in the shade, my sister and I were drifting out of sight.

We ended up smack in front of a massive stone wall with tons of jagged, boulder-size rocks embedded in the sandy ocean floor in front of it. Wedged between two of these rocks was my foot. Somehow I'd managed to get it caught and no amount of pulling by my sister would set it free. All the while the waves were getting bigger, slamming down on us like a liquid hammer. After each crash, the water swelled up above my head before receding and I had just enough time to gasp for a mouthful of air before the next wave was upon me. Then I was under water again, holding my breath, my heart pounding in my ears a mile a minute. Elizabeth would float up and away from me and then, bless her heart, she'd swim as hard as she could back to her task of trying to free me from my rock trap. The waves kept coming closer and harder, and even though I was only eight, I understood that this might be the end for me.

Finally I looked up and saw my father standing on top of that wall. I had never seen such a look of utter panic on his face. Another wave came pounding down on me, and the water swelled up over my head and through my blurry saltwater view, I saw him jump. After leaping in fully clothed, wallet and cigarettes in his pants pocket and watch on his wrist, he swam over and gave me one hard pull. Finally those rocks let go of my foot, which was by then bruised and scraped. All the way back to Aunt Eleanor's my dad ranted passionately about his ruined watch, his soggy wallet, his lack of cigarettes. Nothing about how close he'd just come to losing me. But the look on his face when he appeared on that wall told me all that his words did not. When he'd finished lamenting the collateral damage of the day, he started in about paying more attention to my surroundings, to never swim out of earshot of the lifeguards. He could have saved his breath, though; I was never going back in the ocean again. My newfound swimming skills had nearly gotten me killed, so my love affair with the beach would have to be played out on the shore.

And so it was. We lived in Pittsburgh, a city famous for its three rivers (four if you count the underground one) and no ocean. When we did visit the Atlantic, I'd watch from my towel as my sister would dive for sand dollars. I was so envious. I'd collect shells along the shoreline, but they were not nearly as appealing as those smooth round treasures Elizabeth came back with. She gave me the broken ones. "You'll have to come with me if you want a whole one," she'd say. But every time I'd wade in past my knees my heart would start pounding and I'd begin to have trouble breathing. Panic would set in and I'd hightail it back to safety in the sand. I'd never quite recovered from that near drowning incident. While the rest of my family seemed to enjoy bringing up the hilarity of Dad jumping into the water fully clothed, I was not amused.

The panicky feeling I got when attempting to swim in large natural bodies of water would also overtake me in tight places. I knew that I wasn't likely to drown in a crowded elevator, but that feeling of being surrounded, consumed even, and unable to get out seemed to apply whether there was water present or not. Interestingly enough, I was completely fine in a pool. A fish even. But put me in a lake, a river, or an ocean and I was petrified.

And so for years I watched the swimmers, the boogie boarders, and the surfers—especially the surfers—from my dry towel on the shore. I decided one day, somehow, I was going to try it . . . just as soon as I figured out how to get in past my knees without hyperventilating. By the time I began looking for colleges I knew that there would be one requirement of any school I went to. Despite my fear of swimming in the ocean, I still adored the beach, so it had to be near the coast.

I wanted to be a writer—I couldn't stand anything involving numbers, so it was more than ironic that I ended up at the University of California at San Diego. This is an excellent school, don't get me wrong, but it is known for engineering, math, science, and computer technology. Writing, not so much. What it was to me was geographically desirable. Yes, UCSD is in the beautiful seaside community of La Jolla, California. The fact that it wasn't known for the liberal arts was of little consequence. My dorm had an ocean view.

When I moved in I noticed lots of surfboards. A lot of my dorm mates were avid surfers, and one of my first boyfriends there was a blond San Diego native named Biff. Biff was a fifth-year senior and also a residential advisor. He was supposed to be off limits, or maybe I was supposed to be off limits to him. That only made things more interesting, though. I had high hopes that among the many things I learned from him, surfing would be one of them. But our "relationship" (if you can call sneaking around in the middle of the night a relationship) fizzled fast and I never even got a single lesson.

To tell the truth I could count on one hand the number of times I made it to the beach during my four years at UCSD. Even though it wasn't strong in my major, the classes were really challenging and any free time I did have I spent with my sorority sisters (Delta, Delta, Delta, can I help ya, help ya, help ya?) and my boyfriends. I ended up marrying one of them—he proposed just before I graduated. He'd finished a year ahead of me and once we were engaged we moved to Los Angeles and started working full time. I got pregnant one week after our first anniversary. We had three babies in four-and-a-half years. That kept me extremely busy. Surfing would have to wait.

At least that's what I kept telling myself, justifying the fact that I had still not managed to overcome my anxiety and do what I had come all the way across the country to do. It's not that I hadn't accomplished a lot of other things in the meantime, or that those things weren't important to me. Of course they were. But while I was thoroughly enjoying my busy life, I also was using it as an excuse. I often found myself saying, "I would love to do 'X' one day, it's just that I'm far too busy with the house/kids/hubby. I couldn't possibly fit 'X' in just now. But maybe some day." Right. Someday was increasingly looking like the twelfth of never. My fortieth birthday, however, was looming ever so near.

I erased "learn to surf" from the twelfth of never on my imaginary calendar and wrote it instead on that list of mine—in ink. It wasn't just the surfing I'd hoped to conquer, it was my very well-founded fear of the ocean. Ironically, for all the years I used my family as an excuse not to take a surfing lesson, it was on a family trip that I finally got my chance. Moreover, I wound up doing it with them. I reasoned that if I were going to die, I'd rather do it surrounded by loved ones.

It happened when we were in one of the most beautiful places on earth, Maui. No shortage of surfing spots there. We scheduled a beginner's group lesson for all of us at a highly recommended surf school in Lahaina. Our instructor was a fifty-something Hawaiian named Kimo. For a Hawaiian, he was not very laid-back. He took surfing very seriously and expected us to do the same. He marched us down to the beach single file, the boys both carrying one end of a surfboard under each arm and our daughter, the oldest, my husband, and I all carrying our boards over our heads. Once we got to the sand he taught us the sequence: first, lie belly down on the board, then straighten our arms, arch our backs, and, on his cue, hop our knees underneath us. Next we were supposed to hop up onto our feet and then, finally, stand, knees slightly bent, arms out for balance, and eyes straight ahead. He told us this was the most important thing. "Look at the beach when you're surfing—look where you want to go. If you look anywhere else, *it's all over.*" What was "all over" I wondered? The lesson? That ride? My life? No time to ask, Kimo was already heading out to sea.

We paddled behind him like baby ducks following their mama, and once we were out there he decided our youngest would go first. Most mothers would offer to be the guinea pig in their child's place. I, on the other hand, was still trying to get over the fact that I was in water deeper than my waist. Aidan looked completely comfortable and relaxed. I was nervous on his behalf. I watched as Kimo pushed my baby out into the first strong rideable wave that came along. Aidan looked like a natural as he "popped up" and "hopped" himself onto his knees, then his feet, and then seamlessly stood up on his board. With perfect form he rode his first wave all the way in, jumped off, got back on, belly down, and began to paddle out toward us again. *Show off*, I thought.

Rory and Kayla did almost as well as Aidan. Maybe this was not as hard as I'd thought. Then it was my husband's turn. He, unlike the kids, was not a natural. Growing up he played every sport—but even though he lived most of his life in California, he never learned to surf. I guess it wasn't his thing. He is a big guy—six feet one and just over two hundred pounds—and he's not exactly what I'd call flexible. When he "popped up" and then "hopped" his knees onto the board it did not look seamless like it had when the kids had done it. With all the grace of an elephant he managed to get his feet under himself, but as soon as he tried to stand up he went right over. Uh oh, I thought. My turn.

Kimo went over everything with me one more time before shoving me out onto the next wave. I tried to remember all the steps, but as soon as I hopped from my knees to my feet I just froze. "Stand up! Stand up!" I could hear him yell. But I did not stand. I rode the wave all the way in to shore in a crouched position. As I paddled back to Kimo I watched him send the kids out one after the other again. Again, they made it look easy. Even Kevin managed to stand for a second or two before he fell off his board.

I am nothing if not competitive, so I had to do it this time—I just had to. "Didn't you hear me yelling for you to stand up?" Kimo scolded. "Why didn't you stand up?"

"I don't know," I said honestly. "I just didn't."

"Well this time, when I say 'Stand up,' STAND UP!" And with that he shoved me out onto the next wave. This time I tried not to overthink things. I popped up, hopped my feet underneath myself, getting into in that crouched position again. Damn it! I completely skipped the part where I was supposed to hop to my knees. Oh well, too late. "Stand up! Stand up!" Kimo's voice came like a muffled mantra through the rushing air.

And I did. I stood up. I put my arms out and I kept my knees slightly bent. I was surfing! I was actually surfing! Oh my God, was this a rush or what? I looked around to see if anyone else was marveling at my perfect technique and down I went. I'd taken my eyes off the shore for just an instant and it was all over, exactly like Kimo had said. The problem was, I didn't just fall, I fell and landed butt first on a great big boulder of a rock.

"I'm fine!" I yelled, trying to convince myself that I was. But I wasn't. I was hurt. Badly. Still, I continued surfing for the rest of the hour, refusing to admit that I was miserable. By the end of the lesson, I was in excruciating pain; I'd landed on my tailbone, hard, and in spite of the cold water I felt a hot, sharp twanging pain. Once in the car I finally let go and started crying. My husband was of course shocked when I told him what had happened. "Why didn't you say anything?" he asked incredulously.

"I don't know, I just really wanted to surf, I guess," I said. I didn't want to admit that I was completely humiliated or that I'd wanted to avoid Herr Kimo's reaction if I'd confessed to looking away from shore. Bad enough that I hadn't stood up the first time he'd told me to; I wasn't going to reveal my injury or how I'd come to be injured.

We dropped the kids off at the hotel and off we went to the emergency room. Since Maui only has one hospital, it was pretty crowded. They see people with critical injuries first, and my ass wasn't critical, so I had to wait. "Have a seat," the woman said after collecting my information. Yeah right, I thought. If I could, I wouldn't be here.

I stood there until they called my name and I went in the back. It wasn't any less crowded on the other side of the door; all the curtained-off exam areas were full. I was relegated to a gurney in the hallway where I lay on my side trying to keep my butt covered with the thin hospital gown. Finally a doctor stopped and introduced himself. I explained how I had fallen and landed on my tailbone on a rock. He told me that I might have fractured my coccyx and then with a straight face he told me, "Looks like I'll have to perform a rectal exam."

Right here in the hallway? I thought, my mind racing. *A rectal exam?* This surely could not be right. After he'd walked away I asked my husband to get my cell phone out of my purse. There was a big sign posted on the wall with a picture of a cell phone with a line through it. No cell phones. Fuck that, I thought, and I called my mother. She's a doctor, so I figured she'd tell me this guy was an idiot and that I should just get out of there. "Sounds like you need a rectal exam," she said after I explained the pain and where it was.

"You've got to be kidding me," I told her.

"I wish I was, but that is honestly the best method we have for diagnosing a fracture of the coccyx." Dr. Strangelove came back and told me there was an exam room open. With my husband standing by, I rolled to my side and relented. He explained as he was performing the procedure that he was going to press from the inside and the outside on my tailbone and if it hurt like hell, chances were it was broken. I told him it hurt already without him doing that. As I was trying to talk him out of it, I realized he was already doing it, and it didn't actually hurt that bad. "See? Not broken. Just sprained," he concluded. I had never heard of a sprained tailbone. I was relieved.

"You know," I told him laughing, "Normally I would've expected dinner and a movie first." My funny bone wasn't broken either. On the way back to the hotel I thought about the events of the day. For a minute there I really was surfing. I was out there, one with the ocean, and I loved it. That is, until the ocean reminded me who was in charge. But still, I had pushed past my fear and gotten back in the water. I'd proven to myself that I could do it, even if it was a pain in the ass.

That's not to say that I am completely cured. I still feel nervous when I first get out past where the waves are breaking when I swim in the ocean, and I still don't like to be sandwiched between people on planes or in elevators. The difference now is that instead of giving in to a full-blown, heart-racing panic attack I am able to slow my mind and breathing enough to see that I am in fact, okay, and that what I am feeling is way, way, way beyond what the present situation calls for. The next step is to focus and adjust my reactions so that they line up with my current reality. This is a technique I apply whenever I'm feeling overwhelmed or anxious—not just when I'm feeling claustrophobic. For years there was no getting around my fear of drowning, but I finally worked my way through it—on a surfboard.

#28 ~~Learn to surf~~

. . . .

Surfing helped heal some of my emotional scars, and so did another challenge on my list: horseback riding. By the summer of 1978 my parents' marriage had been over for a couple of years, but I was still suffering from post-traumatic divorce syndrome. That particular summer, my parents were distracted: my father was either busy working—or didn't want to have kids underfoot in his new bachelor pad—and my mother was in China with her medical school studying acupuncture and other ancient Eastern techniques. My sister and I were shipped off to Washington, D.C., to have some quality time with our grandmother, who promptly dumped us off at horseback riding camp. I don't sound bitter, do I?

Anyone who has ever been insane enough to go to D.C. in August knows that it's basically a sauna. And I can tell you that nothing smells worse in a sauna than horseshit. One of our responsibilities as campers was to "muck out the stalls," which is equestrianese for "shoveling shit." It felt like we spent more time cleaning up after the horses than actually riding them. This suited me just fine, however, because while I'd just turned nine, I was the size of a five-year-old. Also, although I loved horses, I was more than a little afraid.

They had assigned to me a giant hulk of a horse called Trotsky, who most likely took one whiff of the fear permeating from my sweaty pores and knew he had it made for the summer. Day after day I nervously got in the saddle (which required quite a lot of help) and attempted to ride that beast around the big ring, English-style no less. I'm not sure why my grandmother, who was from Colorado, would sign us up for English-style horseback riding camp. I'm guessing it had a lot to do with how darling the little black-velvet-covered helmets were and absolutely nothing to do with how stifling hot it was underneath them.

At any rate, Trotsky lived up to his name. He was quite the trotter. He and I both knew who was boss in that relationship, and it wasn't me. Trotsky completely disregarded each and every one of my feeble attempts to control him. He went at what to me was a very scary pace and all the while whipped his head up and down in protest. This made me hold the reins tighter, which caused friction between my sweaty little hands and the leather reins. Every evening, I cried and showed my grandmother the huge fluid-filled blisters that were forming on my tender palms. She was unmoved. Then one day, with one final fling of Trotsky's mighty head, my blisters burst. Both of my hands were bloody and sore before that ride was over.

Instead of pulling me out of camp, my grandmother asked that I be given a different horse. Until my hands healed they put me on a mule and made me go around in circles on a lead line, which was horribly embarrassing. I mean, who goes to horseback riding camp and spends the whole time riding a donkey? Finally they introduced me to a very calm-looking horse with sympathetic eyes named Coffeecake. He was brown. Although I was a bit apprehensive after my experience with the equine dictator, I decided that Coffeecake was a horse I could ride. Coffeecake, unfortunately, did not agree, and made it known by stepping squarely on my foot. People are supposed to break horses, not the other way around. After much swelling and pleading, my grandmother finally relented and I never went back to the camp. I also never got back on a horse.

The fact that I don't ride is beyond ironic given that I live in Hidden Hills. We moved here because of the great sense of community, the beautiful mature pepper-tree-lined streets, and the large lots. It is an equestrian neighborhood with two riding arenas and God knows how many miles of horse trails. I'd been on them many times, on foot. But something about my impending fortieth made me realize it was about time I got back in the saddle. Literally. Yes, it was time for me to tackle another one of those things I "thought I would have done by now" and get my ass back on a horse.

Most of my friends in Hidden Hills have horses, and when I broached the subject, quite a few of them seemed just as enthusiastic about the prospects of me going riding as I did. "You can ride one of my horses!" several of them had exclaimed. And I believe they really meant it. So I waited patiently for one of them to make good on her offer. Weeks went by, months even, and nobody took me riding. I know my friends went riding, sometimes on their own, sometimes with each other. I know because I saw photos they posted on Facebook. I thought by commenting, "WOW—that looks like fun!" that at least one of them would get the hint and invite me along next time. But the invitation never materialized.

I thought maybe if I took initiative and started asking them about specific days that might work, perhaps they'd take me up on it. No such luck. I heard everything from, "I'm just so busy this week," to "I'd love to, but my extra horse has a lame foot right now." I started to get my feelings hurt. Maybe they'd only offered to be nice, and they really didn't want to take me along. I felt about as unwanted and abandoned as I did that summer in D.C., and about as helpless, too. Here I had finally decided to get on a horse, and nobody was helping me do it. My parents, and my grandmother, too, for that matter, were responsible for me that summer back in the day. They, as the adults in my life, were charged with making sure I was safe and cared for and that my needs were being met. But as an adult I was responsible for myself. Why was I still waiting and hoping for someone else to take care of things for me? And more important, why did I feel so bad about myself when they didn't?

Practically the whole summer passed by and I still hadn't gone for a ride. I had, however, spent plenty of time feeling hurt, sad, and dejected. Then August rolled around and we went on that trip to Banff that you read about earlier. In Banff, I'd gone whitewater rafting, ATV driving, and zip-lining, and after each one of these activities I felt really proud of myself. It was a huge confidence booster to learn that I was, in fact, quite capable of doing all of those things. And I got to thinking, sometimes the only way to show yourself that you can do something is to just do it. You can't wait for life to put an adventure in your path; you have to actually pick up the phone and plan it for yourself.

And that's when it hit me: I could apply this same theory of self-reliance to my horseback-riding quest. What was I waiting for? I wasn't a nine-year-old child at the mercy of everybody else's decisions and agendas. One phone call later, I had booked a ride for my family. I'd waited nearly thirty years to get up the nerve to ride again, and then I'd waited all summer for someone else to make sure that happened. But the thing of it is, the only person I really needed was myself. My friends hadn't let me down, I had. There was no reason for me to doubt that they did have the best of intentions when they initially had offered to take me riding. People are busy living their lives, however, and they have plenty of obligations to fulfill already without having to take responsibility for mine, too. Maybe it wasn't so much getting on the horse that should have been my goal as taking the reins and making the ride happen in the first place.

And so, after a lovely brunch at the famous Fairmont Banff Springs Hotel we walked ourselves to the stable right next door (the one I'd called using my very own hands), and the whole family went on a ride. I set out to do it in order to conquer a deep-rooted fear that stemmed from being shipped away to riding camp—a fear of abandonment, a fear of not being able to choose my own destiny. Not a fear of horses. Well, okay . . . maybe a *tiny* fear of horses, I thought, as they brought over a giant gelding. He looked at me with gentle eyes and I gave him a pat as I put one foot in the stirrup and swung my other leg around. "You look like a natural," the stable hand said.

"Let's just hope the horse thinks so," I answered back.

"He's gentle—don't you worry. His name is Tango," the hand laughed, "As in . . . 'Do you want to . . .'" *Don't mind if I do*, I thought, don't mind if I do.

"You sure you don't ride? You look pretty darn comfortable up there," the hand said, as they made some last adjustments and led me over to the line of riders waiting to take to the trails. And I *was* comfortable, too. I leaned down and rubbed Tango's velvety neck. He seemed to know exactly what I wanted of him. It could have been because he'd only gone that exact route hundreds of times already with hundreds of different riders. But I like to think that it was my firm, but gentle hand, and more important, a lack of the very fear that Trotsky had smelled on me all those years ago. It, like Trotsky himself, was ancient history. Tango and I rode right through my leftover pain, my feelings of abandonment, and my fear of horses.

Have you ever felt pain over something in your present that was disproportionate to what was really going on at the time? If so, it might be worth taking a look at the other times in your life you felt that way. Sometimes new situations can trigger feelings about an old one, one that was never really processed or resolved. Oftentimes it was something that happened when you were too young to fully understand the circumstances and know that it was not your fault, or that you couldn't have done anything to change it. When given no explanation, sometimes children think the worst and then internalize it. As they grow, those feelings continue to fester under the surface and leave those pesky emotional scars I keep talking about. The good news is the pain that comes up in our present can help us to heal those wounds from the past. If we recognize them as opportunities to process and grow, they can be seen as positives. For me, the prospect of riding a horse led me to deal with the issues that had kept me from riding one for all those years.

I was able to look back at that little nine-year-old with new wisdom and perspective and let her know that it was all right to be sad about her parents' divorce, that they did love her, and that they didn't mean to abandon her; it was just that they had issues of their own to address. And while it might not have been the best choice for them to leave her at Grandma's that summer, it was in no way because of anything she had or had not done. All the hurt feelings over friends in the present not taking charge of the fulfillment of something on my list had more to do with untrue beliefs about the past than realities of the present. And as much as I was holding on to that identity of the hurt little helpless child, I had grown up and turned out just fine. Not just fine, but capable—capable of leading my own life and giving myself the thumbs up for doing so.

When you make your own list, see if there isn't something on there that you might have put off doing because of pain from the past. And then keep tabs on how you feel as you accomplish your goal. You might find that facing certain activities head on helps you process that pain.

#29 ~~Get back on a horse~~

. . . .

There are things on my list that might, on the surface, seem very trivial and superficial. Take #30, for example: "have a completely organized closet." This challenge consisted of me setting out to conquer clutter and get everything in order so that I might actually wear the pieces that still had tags on them (I sound like a spoiled brat, I know, but please bear with me). In doing so I realized I had a bigger problem than an overstuffed, disorganized closet. I had become a shopaholic. And that merely accounted for the "what," as in, "what" was my problem? And, as my list had taught me, dealing with the "what" without figuring out the "why" does nothing to change patterns and behaviors. Here's the story. I think you'll see what I mean.

I, like so many women, was suffering from a disease that has reached pandemic proportions in the United States. Yes, I admit it. I was a shopaholic. If there is a twelve-step program for this addiction, I didn't know about it. Not that it would have mattered since I was too busy shopping to attend. With shopaholism (as with any other addiction) there is a relentless, ever-pressing need to reach new highs. My disease used to be fed by quick trips to the mall or to local boutiques, but I'd recently graduated to shopping online. Now, online shopping is a very dangerous invention indeed; it makes it entirely too easy to spend, spend, spend. There is no deterrent like, say, having to get dressed and leave the house. One simply has to have a credit card and a PC, Mac, laptop, iPad or iPhone (I've made some of my best purchases on my iPhone).

Well, back to the point. I was a shopaholic. I belonged to seven of those "member's only" shopping sites (yes, I said seven), and all seven of these sites were really savvy when it came to marketing themselves. Almost all of them required me to be "invited" to join by an enabler . . . er . . . I mean current member, which gave me the impression that these were exclusive clubs reserved for only discerning shoppers like myself. They also put a time frame on their offerings. I could get a great price on the latest and greatest designer whatchamacallit but I only had forty-eight hours in which to do it. The sense of urgency heightened with each tick of the clock. And as if that wasn't enough, I could see how many, or more important, how few of the *latest and greatest designer* whatchamacallits there were left. The impulse to snag one of my very own would become too hard to resist, and then before I knew it, my hand was on the mouse. In the blink of an eye I'd make that fateful click and the whatchamacallit was mine.

You really do have to buy fast on those sites. Because even though they claim they are exclusive and reserved for only the crème de la crème, there are actually thousands of other women in their PJ's sitting in front of their computer screens, eyes glassy, hand trembling as it hovers over their mouse. It becomes almost a feat in and of itself just to beat them to the click. And once you've clicked there's no turning back. That item is en route and you cannot return it; you just get store credit and only if they receive it back within thirty days. Some whatchamacallits you can't return at all. It's all in the fine print that I for one wasn't reading because I was too busy trying to beat the other shopaholics to the punch.

I knew I had it bad when I start planning my day around when certain whatchamcallits were scheduled for sale. I signed up for alerts so that I wouldn't miss a single thing. And there were so many things. I was very close to adding "agoraphobia" to my list of ailments if I didn't stop shopping and leave my house. Thank God for laptops and wireless Internet connection, so I could shop online while away from home. The bill for the shrink (for agoraphobia treatment) would've put a serious dent in my shopping budget.

I purchased so many clothes that I didn't even have time to wear them all, or places to wear them all, for that matter. I had shoes, jeans, outerwear, underwear, loungewear, and sportswear that were crowding my closet—many with the tags still on them. Perhaps the saddest sight of all was the cocktail dresses. Oh the cocktail dresses! Like wallflowers at the prom waiting desperately, hopefully, to be asked to dance. I came to the conclusion that I had to stop the madness. I vowed to put my credit card on ice and log off of all of those "exclusive" shopping sites. I figured with all the time I'd have on my hands, I'd go places. Fun places. Places where I could wear a cocktail dress, for example. Yes, I had the wardrobe for doing all kinds of things; to quote an old adage, "If the shoe fits, wear it." That applies to jeans and sweaters, too.

I started the "wear the unworn" process by cleaning out my closet, and that's when I discovered that my closet was magical. It truly was, because what looked like a lot of clothes *in* the closet, looked like enough clothes for ten women *out* of my closet. How did it all fit in there? And moreover, how on earth was it going to fit back in there when I was done sorting it? The sorting was clearly going to take much longer than the hour I'd carved into my schedule to tackle this now daunting task.

There were tall stacks of T-shirts, long sleeve shirts, tank tops, underwear, bras, pajamas, sweaters, jackets, and jeans laid out on every available inch of space on my bed. My two little chairs had completely disappeared under the hanging dresses, slacks, skirts,

and blouses that were stretched over their arms. It looked like someone had taken the entire women's section of a major department
store and dumped it in my room. This was beyond excess.

I began separating the clothes by category, refolding or re-hang-
ing them depending on what they were and how often I wore them.
I found things in there I hadn't seen in ages, that I was completely
unaware I still had, even. That's what happens when the closet is
stuffed so tightly that you can't even see what's in there. I had a few
different piles: one was for throw-away items that were too stained
or stretched out to be of any use to anyone; one was give-away stuff,
things that didn't fit right or that I knew I'd never wear, but that
might look cute on somebody else; and one was for clothes that I was
keeping, a much larger pile than I thought I'd have. Somehow,
things that I hadn't worn or even laid eyes on in three years had a
whole new appeal. Then of course, I had the pile of clothes that still
had the tags on them. I hate to admit how big that stack was; it
looked like I could have opened a boutique or something. These
were, in large part, items I'd ordered online during my many binge-
shopping sessions.

Like any good addict, I immediately started rationalizing my behavior. Some of the clothes were priced so reasonably that I simply
had to buy them. And some of them were so stunningly beautiful on
the models that I simply had to buy them, too. The thing is, though,
that if something is really well priced but isn't something you need,
it's still money spent that didn't need to be spent. Another sad fact of
life, I realized, is that just about *everything* looks stunningly beautiful on a model—because the model herself is stunningly beautiful!
A dress that looks perfect on a 5' 10" frame is not going to necessarily
fit my 5' 3" frame the same way. Ever. Why I am surprised every
time by this, I do not know. Maybe I think I'm still growing.

That doesn't mean the clothes weren't pretty, just that they didn't
hit me in the same places they hit the models. A minidress on them

might be tea length on me. And something that is floor length, well, I'd need stilts to make that work. Basically I needed a good alterations person. Gotta love Facebook, because within minutes of changing my status to read, "I'm looking for a good alterations person," I had several recommendations complete with phone numbers. I called one of them, and she was only too happy to help me, for a price.

I packed all the things that needed to be altered into a giant rolling suitcase. It looked like I was going on a two-week vacation rather than just to Encino. When I started unpacking, the woman's eyes lit up, with dollar signs. For what I paid in alterations I could easily have bought another suitcase full of clothes. But those would need to be altered as well, so I resigned myself to stick with my plan and make these unworn ones wearable.

It took almost two hours for me to try on each thing. I stood still as the tiny woman drew marks with soap and stuck straight pins into dresses, jeans, skirts, etc. When we were through, I was exhausted. I was also excited. As each garment was pinned to its new length, I could see how much more amazing it was and how amazing I would feel wearing it. Now I just had to start thinking of some amazing places to go in all my "new" outfits.

One would think that after having gone to all that trouble and, also, realizing that I had more than one woman could possibly wear, I would've stopped buying more. But I didn't. That's because while I had taken inventory of my closet, I hadn't yet inventoried my psyche. I'd made note of everything I'd bought, but hadn't yet processed *why* I'd bought so much in the first place. I had fessed up to being a shopaholic without really doing anything about it. Like figuring out how I became one. When did this all start and, more important, *why?*

I wasn't always like this. It's not as if I came out of the womb with a tiny credit card or that my first words were, "Charge it!" Not at all.

We had very little money when I was growing up, and given that I had an older sister, most of my clothes were hand-me-downs. After my parents divorced, money was even tighter. My father paid child support, but not alimony, and my mother was a medical student at the time. I think when people hear that my mom is a physician they assume I grew up with a silver spoon in my mouth, or a silver tongue depressor. That couldn't be farther from the truth, though.

My parents got married very young, when my mom was only nineteen, and my dad was twenty-one. They met at George Washington University, where my mother was studying history and hoped to become a teacher. But after they'd been dating for a while, my mom found out she was pregnant with Elizabeth. At the time abortion was illegal, and since my dad seemed to be happy about the pregnancy, they got married and dropped out of school. My mother was going to stay home while my father worked as an engraver in the Pentagon building to support their new family. They lived in first one, and then another tiny house in Alexandria, Virginia, that they shared with some seriously large cockroaches. Then when my dad took a sales job with AT&T, they moved to a slightly bigger house. The cockroaches were the same size, however. That's where they were living when I was conceived.

When I was three, our cousins Michael and Brian came to live with us after their mother, Aunt Ardele, went into an institution to be treated for schizophrenia. The boys were very close in age and only slightly older than my sister Elizabeth. So there were four of us kids, four mouths to feed, four bodies to clothe. My mom was only twenty-five. I know now how difficult it is to maintain a sense of self when you are taking care of everyone else, and my mother hadn't really figured out who she was before she became a parent. Suffice it to say, these were stressful times at my house. After Michael and Brian moved back with their mother, my father was transferred to AT&T's office in Pittsburgh.

So we moved to Pennsylvania, which was when my mom decided it was time for her to go back to school. This time, however, she didn't want to study history; she wanted to be a doctor, which would take two years of undergraduate school followed by four years of medical school and three more years of internship and residency.

I'm sure the strain of her being in school had an effect on my parents' marriage. So did the fact that my father was an alcoholic and my mother is a lesbian. Yes, you read that right. She says that she always knew on some level but didn't really process it until after the divorce. Regardless of when or how she figured it out, it wasn't the only reason for the divorce. You really couldn't pin it on any one thing. Well, you could, but how would you pick which one? I'm surprised that it lasted as long as it did. But this chapter is not about their marital problems, my father's alcoholism, my mother's lesbianism, or their divorce. It's about clothes, or, more accurately at that point in my life, the lack thereof.

My disdain for hand-me-downs only deepened after the divorce. As I said, times were tough and my mom started getting big Hefty bags full of her friend's daughter's cas-offs. Now this girl, Sabrina, was older than Elizabeth, and bigger, too, so what she'd just grown out of usually fit Elizabeth. When Elizabeth was done with whatever it was, I'd get it (or what was left of it). Forget about "sloppy seconds," this was "threadbare thirds."

I got to shop for new clothes twice a year. Just before school started every September I got one pair of school shoes and one pair of gym shoes, both of which were always a half size too big so that I could "grow into them." I had a lot of blisters back then. I also got one new outfit for school. The other time I could purchase something new was right after school let out for summer. Then I could get one new pair of sandals, correctly sized since they only had to last me for a couple of months. Pretty much everything else I wore was a hand-me-down or a handed-down hand-me-down. Most of the time I didn't complain, but once I wrote a letter to my mother, which she kept and gave back to me recently. In it I expressed how much I hated having hand-me-downs and that everything, "smelled like Elizabeth."

Once my mother was a practicing doctor, she started to make a little money. And as soon as I was big enough, I started shoveling people's sidewalks and driveways in the winter and raking leaves from my neighbors' yards in the fall for cash. Back then I was especially good at saving money. I even had a special decorated box for it, along with a little book for keeping track of things. I titled it "Money Matters." Get it? Money *Matters*? The older I got, the more work I could do. I babysat and I worked in my friends' parents' stores: a stationary shop and a baby clothes outfit. At sixteen I got a job as a waitress at the Sichuan House Chinese restaurant in one of the main shopping areas of Squirrel Hill and would go there straight from school on days I had a shift. On days I didn't work, I shopped. I don't know what happened to my little thrifty self, but once I started working the only thing that *mattered* about money was spending it . . . *on clothes*!

What started out with my buying a few items on sale with my own money escalated over the years to become my love affair with online shopping. Maybe it was not so much a love affair as a full-blown addiction. And while this type of addiction didn't involve drugs or alcohol, it certainly involved a need to feel the "high" of making that purchase and my inability to stop going onto those sites in the first place. Yes, I vowed to unsubscribe, but I had only gotten as far as the window that shows the "unsubscribe" box. I couldn't bring myself to click it. That is, until I started working on that list of mine.

Seeing all of those clothes piled around my room and all of those tags still attached to them made me realize just how out of control my shopping had become. I could no longer pretend that my motivation in buying these things was to fill my closet; I had to admit that it was most likely a misguided attempt to fill an emotional need. Could it be that I was trying to help that little girl inside of me to feel like she deserved nice things, that she was not doomed to always wind up with second choice, secondbest, or second hand, just because she'd been born second?

It's entirely possible that as a child I translated my winding up with hand-me-downs into meaning that I was not deserving of something new and special. My efforts to fulfill my need for clothes never satisfied me, because the need wasn't for clothes in the first place, it was for love, confidence, and a sense of self worth. And while I do believe that one can feel good in clothes, the clothes themselves aren't what make you feel good; that comes from the inside. Putting a piece of clothing on the outside doesn't fix a thing if the inside is broken. There is, however, one way that clothes can give you love, confidence and self worth, but it isn't by buying them, or by wearing them; it's by giving them away. With that in mind I set about organizing my closet one more time. This time, my "give away" pile was a lot bigger, my need was much smaller, and my resolve to quit shopping? Strong as an ox.

~~#30 Have a completely organized closet~~

. . . .

Now, I am not an expert in psychology—armchair or otherwise. These are just my own personal stories and observations. When I was making my list I set out to take a surfing lesson, get my ass back on a horse after thirty years, and, of all the superficial things in the world, organize my closet. But in doing those activities I exposed some underlying issues—emotional scars if you will—that I hadn't even realized were there. Something had kept me from doing those things sooner, but what? And once I thought about the what, the why came bubbling to the surface. Until I worked through the why, I couldn't really accomplish the what. Interesting how that works. In the end, when you figure out the why and work through your issues, what you find on the other side is an enlightened, happier, wiser, and better you.

IT'S A TRIP

You know that expression, "Getting there is half the fun"? It doesn't apply to me. That's because I suffer from what I like to refer to as pre-trip anxiety. Other people who are affected by my pre-trip anxiety (namely, my husband, my children, select ticket agents, and flight attendants) would probably call it something else, like stark raving insanity. It's true that I do get a little (ahem) *worked up* before a trip, but in spite of my condition, I included the following travel-related challenges on my list: "get my passport stamped," "plan a girls' getaway weekend," "take the boys camping," and "travel alone."

Just because I wasn't a good traveler didn't mean I didn't want to go places, and there were so many places I had never been. For one, I'd never visited a country that wasn't in North America. I went to Canada as a child (before passports were necessary) and, as a college kid in San Diego, I made the obligatory border crossing into Tijuana, where the drinking age is eighteen. Of course, the tequila prevented me from having much of a memory of being in Mexico. Those were the good old days when American teens could jump across borders, drink themselves silly, and not wind up kidnapped or beheaded—all without need of a passport. And so, I'd never had one.

That was pre-9/11. Now you can't travel anywhere abroad without a passport, and so I decided it was time to get one. I wanted to be free to go anywhere my heart desired. But where was that, exactly? At first I was tempted to put "visit Paris in the springtime" or "see Michelangelo's Sistine Chapel in person" on my list. I'd always wanted to go to Europe (and at the time I am writing this I still haven't been there). But my goal wasn't to visit a particular place; it was to visit *any* place that would earn me that first stamp in my passport. I left out the specifics as to where that could be accomplished, so I'd be free to seize the first opportunity that came my way. This is something that I highly recommend you consider when you're making your own list. Which aspect of the goal you're setting is most important to you? For me, it was getting my passport stamped, and if I'd narrowed my options to just one particular country, it might have been much more difficult to achieve.

Shortly after I obtained my very first passport, my husband and I went to a fundraising auction at our children's school. It was the type of event that begins with a cocktail reception, is followed by wine with dinner, and then, when everyone is good and loose, they start the auction. By then the room is spinning as fast as the auctioneer is talking, and before you know what's happening you're bidding on something you never thought you'd bid on in a million years, like a trip to some island country you've never even heard of in the Caribbean. That's what happened to me, anyway, when my alcohol-induced generosity led me to outbid everyone else for this trip. It didn't even occur to me to find out if airfare was included. Of course, it wasn't. But once the shock of what I'd done wore off, the excitement began to set in. I was going to get my passport stamped!

And so it was that the following June, when the kids were at overnight camp, my husband and I gathered all our mileage and bought tickets to St. Vincent and the Grenadines, a small country in the Lesser Antilles Chain right about where the Caribbean Sea meets up with the Atlantic Ocean. In order to get there we had to stop in Miami and then Barbados, where I got my very first stamp in my very first passport. I got my second one when we landed in St. Vincent. Our resort was on its own island, just a short boat ride from the main island.

Right after we arrived at the resort, a honeymooning couple told us a nightmare of a story about their experience on a day trip into St. Vincent, which involved the locals shouting, "Slut!" at the bride when she walked down the street. Once they arrived at the volcano they'd planned to visit, school-age kids armed with machetes surrounded them. The groom explained that in St. Vincent, if you kill someone with a machete, it's not considered murder. I don't know if this is true or not. I didn't want to take any chances.

So we stayed trapped on tiny Young Island like castaways. Our little cottage on the beach was somewhat rustic. The shower was outside, and the old polyester bedding looked like it hadn't been cleaned in decades. There was no television, no Internet, and no air-conditioning, but there was a ceiling fan and French doors that opened onto the beach. This would have been wonderful, except there was a man who would come and sit right outside of those French doors to get what little shade he could from a palm tree while he waited to rent kayaks to guests. Although I never saw a single taker, the man remained parked there all day, every day of our vacation.

The resort may have been short on privacy, but there was one thing it had an abundance of—insects. Our little cottage on the beach was home-sweet-home to a very large, and very hungry, mosquito population. At the end of the third day I counted twelve bites on one leg and eleven on the other. In spite of our six-legged roommates and our unexpected abstinence from electronics we managed to have a very nice time reading and relaxing. The meals were included as part of the package and the food was very good. They had the most amazing breads, which were baked fresh daily and brought out to the tables on long wooden boards. Although I did my best to counter the carbo-loading with hiking and swimming, I still gained two pounds. But I didn't care, because I also gained two stamps in my slightly less stiff-and-shiny passport.

#31 Get my passport stamped

. . . .

Getting my first passport stamped was an important goal on my list in part because most of my friends had passports and had traveled somewhere, and I didn't like feeling left out. Something else that most of my friends had done, but I hadn't, was go away on a girls' getaway weekend.

In high school I was a floater, meaning that I wasn't a core member of any particular group. Instead, I had friends in all of them. It was great in the sense that there was always someone to sit with at lunch, but not so great when people had small get-togethers or outings. I wasn't usually a close enough friend to be invited to those.

Not much changed after I grew up. So I would listen politely to women talk about all the fun they had on weekends away spent with their best friends, and try very hard not to be jealous. Of course, I was jealous anyway. When I was thinking of things to include on my list, "plan a girls' getaway weekend" came to mind. It was high time I stopped being jealous of these women who "have girlfriends, will travel," and became one of them.

It was spring of 2010 when I was sitting at my computer, staring in disbelief at an amazing rate on a room at the Ojai Valley Inn and Spa. Even though I'd sworn off Internet shopping, I went ahead and bought it. I figured since it was such a great price, and that I planned to use the room to accomplish a goal from my list, that it was justifiable. And so I clicked my mouse and called someone who by then had become one of my closest girlfriends: Nancy.

This is the same Nancy from my "invite someone I don't know well, but whom I admire to lunch" challenge. I gained a lot from that lunch, like the opportunity to achieve several other goals from my list. More important, I gained a very good friend. We have similar backgrounds, similar interests, similar senses of humor and style, and both of us love to write. We also are both very good at convincing our husbands to do things for us, like watch the kids, and so there we were, two women of leisure, ready for adventure. It would be the perfect girls' getaway weekend.

And it started out to be exactly that. When we got to Ojai, the bees were buzzing, the flowers were blooming, the trees were budding, and the pollen was plentiful. I myself do not suffer from seasonal allergies, but Nancy does. A fact she might not have been aware of prior to our foray into Pollenville. When I picked her up on Saturday morning, she had a little puffiness under her right eye. It was certainly nothing to worry about. Or so we thought. We drove to Ojai with the top down on my convertible. Very Thelma and Louise of us, I thought. In hindsight, that was a bad idea. We didn't know then that our heaping order of fresh air came with a side of pollen.

By the time we got to Ojai, Nancy had a tiny case of the sniffles. Still, we didn't think much of it. We walked around and peeked into shops. Maybe we did a bit more than peek. We each bought a necklace, I found a darling lacy blouse, and Nancy got a very hip white leather jacket. We ate lunch on the patio of a lovely local restaurant. It was late afternoon by the time we arrived at the Inn.

The Ojai Valley Inn & Spa is beautiful. The grounds are spectacular, chock-full of purple and silvery-gray lavender, Mexican sage, and a variety of other native plants, trees, and shrubs, all meticulously designed to seem as if they just grew there spontaneously. Scattered throughout the property are clean white stucco buildings with terra-cotta tile roofs. Nancy and I were awash in a feeling of serenity as we drove up the long driveway and headed to the reception area.

Unfortunately that feeling of serenity was quickly replaced with frustration because just as I had found this ridiculously great rate online, so had hundreds of other bargain-hunting shopaholics. The resort was filled to the gills, and the spa was completely booked. "So you are telling me that we spent all this money, managed to convince our respective husbands to pull kid duty, drove up here to the Ojai Valley Inn & *SPA*, and we cannot have any *SPA* treatments?" The front desk clerk apologetically, yet firmly, confirmed that yes, we had. Furthermore, the room was nonrefundable, and the reservation was unchangeable. We were stuck.

We decided to make the most of it. If we couldn't indulge ourselves at the spa, then we would just have to indulge ourselves with an amazing feast at the Inn's renowned Maravilla Restaurant, right? Wrong. The restaurant was also completely booked. Deflated, we got into the waiting golf cart and were shuttled off to our room. Things started to look up the second we opened the door. The room was our own little Shangri-la, complete with fireplace, soaking tub, and an amazing view of Ojai's majestic mountains. It was both elegant and casual, decorated with beautiful paintings and fabrics created by local artisans. We propped open the door to the balcony to enjoy the lovely breeze. We ordered room service. After a nice glass of chardonnay and what turned out to be a perfectly wonderful meal of salmon, roasted veggies, salad, and crème brûlée, we decided to call it a night. Surely by morning we'd have a newfound bounce in our pedicure-less step. All we needed was a good night's sleep.

We did not get one. The second the lights were out I heard a noise coming from the other side of the bed and realized that my dear friend Nancy was snoring. Loudly. I wish you could see how petite this woman is. The oddity of such a big, deep noise coming from such a delicate little woman surely must be one of the great ironies of nature. I am no stranger to snoring. If snoring were an Olympic sport, my husband would have four gold medals for it, one for every Olympics held since we got married. He never snored before then—which I believe was some sort of evil plot of his. Get the woman to say "I Do" before unleashing the unholy demon sounds that will haunt her sleep for all eternity. He sleeps in the guest room more often than not now. There's only so much a girl can take. I'm a light sleeper to begin with, and believe me, I've tried everything invented to block out that noise to no avail. Vacations together are the opposite of restful for me. It's too expensive to book separate rooms so I resort to earplugs, pillows over my head, and sleeping pills, but I still come home looking like the star of *Dawn of the Dead*.

And that's probably how I looked on that bright Sunday morning in Ojai. I didn't get a single wink of sleep on my getaway with Nancy. She snored and snored, and I tossed and turned. I got up to look for my trusty earplugs, but wouldn't you know it, I hadn't packed them. I had no idea that I'd need them since I'd left that grizzly bear hubby of mine at home. I used the cotton balls the resort had provided, but still I couldn't sleep. I put a pillow over my head. Nope, didn't work. Finally I climbed out of that extremely comfortable 600-thread-count-sheeted four-poster bed and lie down instead on the cold tile floor in the bathroom. I used a bathrobe (also provided by the resort, although probably not for this purpose) as a blanket and shut the rather heavy pocket door that separated me from the thundering racket.

I could still hear it but, somehow, just enough of the noise was absorbed by the wooden door and I finally, thankfully, fell asleep. Until Nancy woke up in the middle of the night to discover that I wasn't in the bed anymore, that is. She slid the pocket door open and stood over me asking, "What on earth are you doing in here on the floor?"

"I love you Nancy, but you snore," to which she replied, "NO-BODY has *EVER* said that I snored before!" Really? Hmmm. Well, I know I probably should have felt honored to be the first at something, but all I felt was pain. My shoulder and hip were killing me. That hard tile floor was, well . . . hard. I assured Nancy that I would not have gone in there to sleep like that for the fun of it, and that yes . . . she snores, loudly, like a contented pirate.

"I'll fix it! I promise! Go lie down in the bed!" I was skeptical, but my hip and shoulder really couldn't take another hour on that tile floor. So I climbed back into the bed cautiously and crossed my fingers. Nancy reemerged with a scarf of some kind tied around her face—her theory being that if she could prevent her mouth from dropping open, she would not snore. That was the theory. But the theory was disproved very quickly as she resumed the snoring and I resumed the listening to the snoring.

In the morning neither of us looked too hot. Her eyes were puffy from allergies. Mine were puffy from what I am now calling "secondhand allergies." It's kind of like how a nonsmoker gets lung cancer from being around someone who smokes. Her allergies were bothering her, and she was bothering me. After breakfast the two of us went to the store and bought some Zyrtec and hydrocortisone cream for Nancy. There was really nothing to buy for me, as secondhand allergies are untreatable—untreatable, but not *unpreventable*.

From now on if I ever go on a girls' getaway again I'll remember to request a doctor's note stating that said girlfriend is allergy-free or adequately dosed up with antihistamine.

An early morning bike ride, a brisk hike, maybe a swim—those were our big plans for Sunday, but that was before the chainsaw festival that took place in our room all night Saturday night. In my state of sleep deprivation, any attempt at biking and hiking and swimming would have resulted in crashing and falling and drowning (oh my!). And since my mind was basically mush, writing was most definitely out of the question. Nancy tried teaching me the art of transcendental meditation. But I was too tired and stressed out to concentrate on relaxing. What I needed was a drink.

And that's when it hit me. We could go wine tasting! Wine tasting didn't require any physical exertion or mental sharpness, *and* it was on my list! I'd never gone before and I'd heard there was a vineyard somewhere around Ojai. Unfortunately, I'd heard wrong. My dreams of Nancy and I rolling up our sleeves and picking the fruit from the vine and then stomping on it barefoot à la Lucy and Ethel were dashed. But just because nobody in Ojai was growing grapes themselves didn't mean nobody was making wine. And what do you do with wine once it's made? You *taste* it. We didn't really need a vineyard, what we needed was a winery, or, as it turned out, *a bar*, that doubled as a tasting room, the Casa Barranca Winery Tasting Room & Gift Gallery to be exact.

We came across it as we strolled sluggishly up and down Ojai Avenue. I wanted to taste some wine, and taste some wine I did, lots of it. We opted for the Chiefs Peak Flight. A *flight*, I found out, was a grouping of wines to be tasted. See? I learned something about wine before I'd even tasted any. It's not that I'd never tasted any wine before; I grew up half Jewish so there was Manischewitz at Passover and Yom Kippur. Or was that Purim? I don't recall. I'd also had wine at dinner parties (other people's as well as my own) but I pretty much stuck to house Chardonnay or whatever was on sale at Vons. My husband gets headaches from the sulfides in reds, so I also avoided them out of solidarity. But this was my chance to get in touch with my inner wine snob—I mean *oenophile* (see, I really did learn something!).

We bellied up to the bar, plunked down $15, and the very cute and very young guy behind the bar started to pour. I know he said his name, but I do not remember it. The question as to whether to spit or swallow is always an awkward one—and yes, I'm still talking about wine. I gingerly broached the subject and was instructed that if I didn't like the selection I could just spit it into my glass and pour it into one of the wooden buckets set up on the bar for just that purpose.

First up in the Chiefs Peak Flight was a 2008 Grenache from the Santa Barbara Highlands Vineyard. Now you might be wondering how I remembered that when I could not remember that darling bartender boy's name. Simple. I took notes. Yes. I took careful notes that started out really neat and legible and ended up something resembling loopty loops and chicken scratch. That may have been because nameless bartender boy was a generous pourer and I was a shy spitter, as in, I did not spit at all. I swallowed so as not to risk offending the nameless bar boy. Still talking about wine. I imagined that he had picked the grapes, made the wine, bottled it, and lovingly glued the labels on the bottles by hand. I didn't want him to think that I didn't appreciate his efforts.

According to the bar boy the Grenache was "a Spanish grape with the perfect blend of masculinity and femininity." So the wine was a hermaphrodite? According to me the Grenache "burned my throat a bit," and, "was not sweet." That's what I wrote in my notes, anyway. Then came a pinot noir from the La Encantada Vineyard in Santa Rita Hills. This one was "also not sweet, but lighter than the Grenache." After that my notes got a little more lowbrow. The

Bungalow Red from Santa Barbara County was "sweeter, better than the first two," and of the Arts & Crafts Red from the Central Coast I wrote: "smelled like rubbing alcohol." The final selection was a merlot from the Santa Ynez Valley in Santa Barbara about which I wrote, "Good, but not as good as the Bungalow Red."

When it comes to things like shoes or jewelry, if you line up one hundred items, I will pick out the most expensive one. This gift (or curse, depending on who you ask) does not transfer to wines, however. The Bungalow Red, my favorite of all of the wines I tasted, was the cheapest. Not only that, it wasn't even a straight out type of wine. It was a blend of different wines. Probably the ones left over that weren't good enough to be classified as merlot or pinot noir. I picked the mutt of the wine world, the common table wine.

Oh well, no matter. It still gives you a pretty good buzz. Thus concluded our wine tasting excursion. As I slid off of my stool and started to weave across the floor toward the door the cute bar boy called out a warning, "Don't drive for a while. Don't even hold your car keys in your hand as you walk around. The cops here arrest people for having the 'intention to drive under the influence.'" Turns out the woman one stool over from me had been arrested for that very offense the weekend prior. Can you believe that? How do the cops know whether you really were intending to drive drunk? Some people just like to carry keys around. But I did not want to risk it.

Luckily, right next to the Casa Barranca Winery-Tasting Room & Gift Gallery was an ice cream shop. I opted for the Maple Walnut flight. I did not take the time to jot down notes about my ice cream selection. I was too busy devouring it. But I remember it as "creamy, sweet, and delicious." I was pretty sure the cops, as much as they must have very little to do there in Ojai, were not going to arrest me for "Walking While Euphoric."

There is something about alcohol and sugar that makes everything better. We may have been exhausted and somewhat stuffy, but we managed to have an incredible time anyway. It was the kind of adventure that I'd always hoped to have, a real "girls' getaway." I don't know why on earth I never had a getaway before. But one thing's for sure: I'll be doing it again very soon. In the end it didn't matter whether we had spa appointments, or reservations in a fancy restaurant, or even sleep or antihistamines. We had each other, and that's all we really needed. But next time I think I'll bring my earplugs, just in case.

#32 ~~Plan a girls' getaway weekend~~
#33 ~~Go wine tasting~~

. . . .

At The Ojai Valley Inn & Spa I experienced luxury. Better yet, I experienced it on an honest-to-goodness girls' weekend and at a very reasonable online deal of a price. When I was growing up we didn't take vacations to luxury resorts. We went camping. I loved sleeping in a tent, the smell of campfire, toasting marshmallows on sticks, going fishing and crabbing, and seeing all the stars in the sky.

After my parents were divorced I continued to go camping. I went with my mother and her girlfriend who had grown up in Tennessee and was a pretty good outdoorsman, I mean outdoors*woman*. I also went camping with my father and stepmother. My stepmom Margie was not an outdoorswoman. What Margie was, was organized. Camping trips with my mom and her girlfriend usually involved a tarp, a tent, sleeping bags, a duffel bag of clothes, toilet paper, and a cooler containing milk, eggs, a loaf of bread and a pack of hot dogs, and maybe a can of beans or two. Trips with my stepmother included everything but the kitchen sink. She didn't need to bring that because she found some kind of portable one specifically designed for camping.

Margie used to pack the Jeep so full that she couldn't see out the rear window. Then she found out about the *Ex-Cargo*. That amazing invention looked like a giant Big Mac container. It attached to the roof of the Jeep, allowing Margie to bring even more stuff. She had a coffeepot, a propane stove, pots and pans, a plastic bin in which to wash all the pots and pans, tin plates, cups, and utensils, air mattresses, sleeping bags, pillows, camp chairs, a portable radio, board games, cards, clothing for every climate, biodegradable shampoo, conditioner, soap, a solar-heated water dispenser so we could shower in warm water (in case there wasn't a good enough bathroom facility), a hair dryer, curling brush, and makeup (in case there was), bug spray, sunscreen, aloe vera, Solarcaine, Calamine lotion, a first-aid kit, and a couple of coolers full of food—I'm not just talking about hot dogs, but everything to make cheese omelets, pancakes, sandwiches, soup, spaghetti and meatballs, salad, burgers, etc. This was just to supplement the meals we made from what we caught when we went fishing, crabbing, and clam digging. In other words, the woman came prepared.

Our fishing, crabbing, and clamming activities came with a certain degree of danger. For instance, once when we went camping in Nova Scotia and took pails down to the red rocky beach of the Bay of Fundy to dig for clams, I quickly got bored and set out to find amethysts, which were rumored to be all over the place there. The Bay of Fundy tides change in a heartbeat and the beach disappears in a flash when they do. In spite of all the warnings we got from well-intentioned locals with their funny pseudo-Scottish accents to "Beware the high tide in the Bay of Fundy," we, of course, got stuck. We waded in waist-deep water (not easy to do while holding a full bucket of clams over your head) until we finally found a climbable section of the cliff. I never did find a single amethyst, but we did manage to hold onto most of our clams. I must say that the chowder we made on the Coleman stove in one of Margie's special camping soup pots using the cream and potatoes, celery, salt, and pepper she'd brought from home was the best I've ever tasted. Once we were out of the wet clothes and warmed up by the campfire enjoying our well-earned clam chowder, we were happy as . . . well . . . *clams.*

Another time when we were camping on Chincoteague Island in Virginia, we set traps with raw chicken necks tied inside (to lure the crabs) and then went fishing on the dock. More often than not, the crabs that didn't want the chicken necks would go after the bait on the hooks of our poles. We had to check often to see if we needed to re-bait. One day I was reeling in my line to do just that when my stepmom came up behind me and pulled my face backward in order to slather it with sunscreen. In spite of my protests she was determined to cover my entire face, including my eyes. And so I couldn't see when the line came up out of the water that a massive crab was busily munching what was left of the bait on the other end. This must have been the granddaddy of all crabs—the crab that ate all the other crabs—that's how big he was.

Everyone was whispering excitedly, "Get the net, get the net!" and I was still there, head back, eyes closed, face covered in sunscreen. My stepmother let go of my face and took the net from my father and attempted to get it under that crab. I frantically wiped my eyes with my sleeve and opened them just in time to see her accidentally hit the crab with the net and knock it off my line. It disappeared under the water and for the rest of that trip my dad would not stop teasing my stepmother about it. I tried to re-catch that crab every day, several times a day, with no luck. It will forevermore be my "one that got away." It was of little consolation that I didn't get sunburned on that trip.

I always assumed that when I had kids I'd take them camping. But at the time I made my list we'd gone just once, years earlier, when Kayla's preschool planned a camping trip. I was so excited that I went out and bought every possible piece of camping gear manufactured, including a cooler, plastic utensils, aluminum cookware, biodegradable soap, lanterns, propane stove, tents, tarps, air mattresses, and pumps for the air mattresses. I had enough supplies for a lifetime of camping trips. But, after that one, we never went again. Maybe it was too ambitious to try to camp with a preschooler, a toddler, and a baby on the way. It was a lot of fun, but it was also a lot of work. I was exhausted for an entire week after one weekend of roughing it.

By the time I made my list, though, my kids were older and I was definitely not pregnant, and I decided it was time to give camping another try. My daughter was working as a CIT at an overnight camp and my husband had to work, so it would just be me and the boys. Since we were going to be on our own, I started rethinking the whole pitching of the tent part of camping. I'd heard of a campground that had tents set up and ready to go and upon further investigation I found that they also had small cabins. My boys balked a bit, saying that it wasn't really camping if we weren't going to be sleeping in a tent. I did my best to convince them that it was still going to be rustic enough to count as camping and promised them that we'd do all of our cooking outside on the campfire. I was willing to forgo using the kitchenette, but the bathroom was a different story. I realized that this may make me sound soft, but I can live with that.

We arrived at El Capitan Canyon and checked into our creekside double—sounds like a drink doesn't it? "I'll have a creekside . . . make it a double . . . on the rocks!" By the end of the first day I could have used one.

After we'd unpacked our stuff and settled into our cabin, we decided to trek down to El Capitan State Beach. It was not a far walk, but for kids who never walk anywhere (we live in L.A.; people drive from one end of a parking lot to the other while running errands in the same shopping center), it was quite a hike. There was a lot of moaning and groaning and cries of "Are we there yet?" The beach was fun while it lasted, which was about forty-five minutes. It was already 3 p.m. when we got there, and it was pretty chilly. The kids braved the freezing water and made the best of it, I'll give them that. The beach itself was rather narrow and the small amount of sand there was to lay the towels on was quickly disappearing as the tide came in. So we packed up and walked back to our campground.

After we'd all showered, I went about getting the charcoals going for the big event: cooking dinner outside. We had a round fire pit with a grill that covered half. I put a pile of charcoal on the side with the grill and made a fire with firewood on the other side. I told the boys that everything tastes better when you're camping. I don't know if that's true or if they just fell under the influence of that notion, but those boys polished off an entire package of turkey hot dogs, half a dozen tortillas (great on the grill with melted cheese), salad, corn on the cob, a potato, applesauce, and for dessert, s'mores.

We cleaned up and hung out for a bit outside before turning in for the night. The boys watched a DVD on my laptop and I read from my Kindle. So you can see, we weren't entirely "unplugged," but since both gadgets were running on battery I decided to let it slide. Plus, I wanted to catch up on my reading, and letting the boys watch a movie was the only way that was going to happen. Before we went to sleep they both proclaimed it to be the best vacation they've ever taken inside of California. Too bad that didn't last.

In spite of the fact that we were in beds and not on a hard ground in sleeping bags, none of us got any sleep. There were too many strange noises outside. We heard the usual crickets and owls, but also some unidentified (but potentially dangerous—you never know!)

animals, too. We eventually gave up, around 7:30, and made our breakfast outside. After that I figured we'd go horseback riding or ocean kayaking. But the boys didn't want to do either. I could hardly believe it. They dismissed every idea I came up with, but finally, they reluctantly agreed to a bike ride. The place has a ton of bikes you can borrow. Problem is, they are all adult size. Rory could manage. Aidan, though? Not so much. Of course this led to a fight because Aidan was angry that there wasn't a bike for him, and Rory was angry that even though there was one he could ride, he wouldn't be riding it. I explained that we were there to spend time doing something together even if we all hated it, which it looked like we were destined to do.

We ended up taking a hike to what was advertised as a llama farm. I imagined a whole herd of soft and friendly llamas roaming around a beautiful open meadow waiting to be petted and maybe even fed by visitors like us. But I was wrong.

The "hike" took us past an organic farm. Not organic llamas, but organic vegetables or herbs of some kind. I can't be sure because we couldn't get close enough to see what was growing. There were barbed-wire fences all around the edge and migrant workers toiling away. I started to feel bad and wondered how much these guys were getting paid to be hunched over all day tending to whatever it was they were tending to and being gawked at by pseudo-campers like us, who had meandered up there expecting to see llamas. But as we got higher up the hillside we saw there actually were llamas. Real live llamas! And they looked very soft and cute in the distance, but once again, they were fenced in by barbed wire and we couldn't get anywhere near them. Needless to say the boys were not pleased. I heard a lot of "I can't believe we walked all the way up here for nothing," on the way back down the hill.

I tried to spin it as best I could. "Sometimes life is about the journey and not the destination," I quoted.

They countered with, "Well the journey sucked." It was pretty much true.

"It was something to do anyway," I said. But what else was I going to do to fill this, our second and only full day? I offered to take them back to the beach again. No sale. I suggested swimming in the campground's heated pool. Again, no sale. In the end we did what we often do when we have time on our hands at home. We went to the movies. Yes, I drove out of the campground and down the freeway to civilization and we went to a movie theater. So much for being one with nature.

When we got back to our campsite it was time for dinner. I lit the fire and we grilled steaks and ate the rest of the corn, some beans, and more tortillas. It seemed the most successful part of the trip was going to be the cooking part. They ate well and we tried our hand at telling ghost stories. Unfortunately, we really didn't know any. So we headed inside our cabin and watched another movie on my laptop. I'd only brought it so that I could get some writing done, but it seemed like that was not in the cards. Speaking of cards, why didn't I think to bring a deck of those?

We slept better that night, and I was hopeful that our third and last day would be the best one yet. No such luck. After breakfast we went to the pool and within minutes the fights began. I think my kids can only play together for so long before it turns physical and then inevitably one gets hurt and then they fight. I kept on saying, "Stop that" and "What did I tell you about that kick board?" and "Stop trying to push your brother underwater." Finally I decided I'd had enough and I ordered them out of the pool and marched them back to the cabin. I packed up our stuff and we headed home. I felt like an utter failure.

I'd had such high hopes for this camping experience; I wanted it to be just like when I was little. But then I started trying to remember exactly how that was for me. I had to admit that although my memories of camping with my family are fond, they aren't all good. Remember the beginning of this chapter, where I described almost drowning in Nova Scotia and missing out on catching the crab of a lifetime due to parental-inflicted blindness by sunscreen? Funny now, yes. Funny then? Not one bit. And come to think of it, when things weren't super-exciting in a bad way, they were often boring. I remember having plenty of time to kill, and I killed it by reading by myself.

My sister and I were hardly best friends. We did play together sometimes, but there were lots of times when we fought, just like my boys do. My parents rarely got involved until blood was shed. Then they'd separate us, threaten to spank us if we carried on, and go back to whatever it was they were doing before we had so rudely interrupted them. Maybe I shouldn't have tried to force my boys to get along. If peace was achievable just by ordering people to stop fighting, then there wouldn't be any problems in the Middle East now, would there? Maybe I should have separated the boys for a bit and had them play apart until they were ready to come together again.

And as for the disagreement over what to do, I seem to recall that when I was little my family was run less like a democracy and more like a dictatorship. The parents were the dictators and we were the followers—and we followed, or else. I'm not saying I want to go all Mussolini on my kids or anything, but I could have put my foot down and just told them, "Today we are going kayaking," and tuned out any flack that might have followed. I know in the end they would have enjoyed it, even if they didn't want to do it in the first place. And even if they didn't enjoy it, it wouldn't have killed them.

In spite of how many lows there were on this trip, there were still some real highs. And those were the only parts the boys told their dad about when we got home. "They didn't mention the fighting? Or the boredom? Or me *kinda* wigging out?" I asked, shocked.

"Nope. They both said they had a great time. They loved the beach, the cooking outside. Oh—and the llamas! You saw llamas on a hike?" Interesting how they'd edited out the negative parts of the trip and focused on the positive, just like I had when I was their age. I decided to do the same and concluded that the camping adventure hadn't been a bust after all. It was something I'd wanted to do for years, as evidenced by the fact that it ended up on my list. I'd committed myself to doing it and fulfilled that commitment. That alone made the trip a success. The fact that the boys came away with a good, albeit edited, memory of the experience was icing on the cake.

#34 ~~Take the boys camping~~

. . . .

So far the travel-related challenges on my list all included other people. I got my passport stamped with my husband; I went on my girls' getaway and wine tasting trip with my friend Nancy; and I went camping with the boys. But what I hadn't done yet was take a trip by myself. Why would I have put "travel somewhere alone" on my list? Simple. I hadn't had much "me time" since having the kids. I was completely out of touch with my own personal clock; it seemed that everything I did was at the mercy of someone else's schedule.

I wanted to see what it would feel like to wake up when I was ready to wake up, not when I had to because breakfasts needed to be made and lunches had to be packed. I wanted to eat when I was hungry and not when it fit in between soccer practice and homework hours. I wanted to go to sleep (or nap for that matter) when I was tired, not because I knew I had to be up and at 'em again in seven hours. The only way to get off of everyone else's time clock was to physically remove myself from the house. I would have to go somewhere else, and I would have to go there alone.

As with the Ojai weekend, I fell off the online shopping wagon again and bought the vacation package on the Internet. It was yet another online offer that I couldn't refuse. I'd put traveling alone on my list, which, in my view, was the same as having a permission slip written and signed by me saying that I was allowed to make that purchase and take that trip.

Brace yourself for a moment because this is going to sound really decadent. I went to Kauai. Yes. For the same money it would've cost me to go stay at a hotel in L.A., I booked a room at the Princeville Resort in Kauai. Since I used mileage for my plane ticket I was able to swing it.

And I didn't really need to spend money on anything except food when I was there because I didn't do anything. That's right. I didn't go on any tours, or whale watching, or scuba diving. I'd gone there to be alone and not have to follow a schedule, and that's what I did. I was worried at first that I'd be bored, but that wasn't the case. I filled my time reading, walking, sleeping, watching the waves, and writing. In fact, I got a lot of writing done while I was there. I'm most productive when I'm able to focus on one task at a time. If you have children, you know this is nearly impossible at home. Even when my kids are at school, I have to be a multitasking machine in order to keep up with all the household responsibilities.

In the past I didn't feel comfortable taking time away from my family to do something like that. I felt selfish and guilty about leaving them behind. I also wondered how on earth the family would function if I wasn't there to manage everything. This is a common problem mothers have. We think that we alone are the ones keeping all the balls in the air and that if we're out of the picture, some of those balls might drop. Things don't get done exactly the same way as when we're the ones doing them, that's true. But they do get done.

If you have someone you trust to man the ship, whether it's a husband, a partner, a friend, a family member, or a babysitter, I highly recommend you disappear for a weekend. Leave someone else in charge and you'll see that everyone can and will survive without you. Plus, if it's a husband or partner you're leaving in charge, it gives them a chance to feel capable with the kids, and also to know just what it is that you do all day. They will most likely be impressed with all that you manage and be extra appreciative when you get home.

If you don't have someone with whom you can entrust the kids, then see if you can bribe them into letting you have a couple of hours to yourself. I'm not suggesting that you leave them home alone, but perhaps you can convince them to watch a video or do a craft project while you get an hour of "me time." You can use it any way you'd like. Take a bath, listen to your favorite music, catch up on your reading, anything. Don't let anything interrupt you; unless someone is seriously having an emergency, they shouldn't disturb you during this time. If the kids are too young to be unsupervised, then maybe wake them an hour early one morning and then put them to bed an hour early that night. Then use that extra hour to do something that's just about you. It's like hitting an imaginary reset button, but with very real results.

#35 Travel somewhere alone

. . . .

Taking on my travel challenges taught me some valuable lessons. First of all, I am not a good traveler, and no matter how many trips I take, abroad or otherwise, that is not going to change. I will always have a certain amount of pre-trip anxiety. It's part of my charm.

Anyone who is close to me will just have to learn to appreciate it as such.

While I am a creature of habit in general, I still have a spontaneous side. It may have taken a few drinks too many, and a fast-talking auctioneer to bring it out in me, but it does indeed exist. Spontaneity doesn't have to equal stupidity; I was smart enough to know not to venture out among machete-wielding tourist-haters.

I shouldn't wait around for someone to ask me to go on a girls' getaway, or to go anywhere else for that matter. If I want to go somewhere with a friend, all I have to do is ask someone. For all I know she is sitting there wondering why I never invite them along. If we're sharing a room, I should always ask first if they snore. If they say no, I should bring earplugs anyway. Just because I have a new appreciation for wine doesn't mean I have a new level of tolerance to it. Also, liking the blended variety doesn't mean I have poor taste. It just means I get to enjoy wine *and* save money for more important things, like ice cream, which serendipitously goes great with blended reds.

You know what else would probably go great with blended reds? Camping! I'll have to remember to bring some wine next time, along with cards, our bikes, books, and one-player games. I also have to remember that camping with my kids won't be a rerun of some romanticized version of my childhood experience. It will be an entirely new experience that my own children get to romanticize any way they want.

Last, it's important to have some new experiences of my own, and the best way to do that is to go somewhere by myself. It's not selfish. It's actually the opposite since I will come home with renewed energy and excitement about life that I can share with my family. This does not require any set amount of time or distance. Even an hour to myself in the other room can do wonders.

ELEVEN

I'LL HAVE WHAT SHE'S HAVING

I used to watch other people enjoying things that just didn't appeal to me and wonder, *am I missing something here?* Sometimes I would make a mental note to give one of these activities a shot at some future date. When I made my list, that nonspecific future date hadn't yet arrived, and it probably never would have, either. The list gave me an opportunity to give something new a whirl, and so I put down a few of those pastimes I knew other people loved doing, but that I had not yet tried myself. These were "watch some of the old classic movies," "be a sports fan," and "go paddle boarding."

· · · ·

The movies I remember seeing when I was growing up were not exactly "classics." Except maybe *Star Wars*, but mostly everyone's seen *Star Wars* so it didn't feel like it counted. At any rate, I saw things such as, *The Muppet Movie, Nine to Five, Fletch, Flashdance, Beverly Hills Cop, Lethal Weapon,* and *Three Men and a Baby.* Naturally, I saw anything by John Hughes starring Molly Ringwald, which was pretty much every movie he made during the 1980s. Please don't think I have one negative word to say about the work of the late, great John Hughes. *The Breakfast Club*, *Pretty in Pink*, and *Sixteen Candles* will always be some of my all-time favorites. Still, you know that expression, "They don't make 'em like they used to"? I figured that this must apply to movies just like it seems to apply to everything else. In fact, I wouldn't be at all surprised if that expression came from a classic film.

How many times have you heard somebody quote a line from *Casablanca* ("Of all the gin joints in all the towns in all the world, she walks into mine;" "Here's looking at you kid;" "Round up the usual suspects"); *All About Eve* ("Fasten your seat belts, it's going to be a bumpy night."); or *On the Waterfront* ("I could have been a contender.")? When I created this challenge, I'd never seen any of those films. I'd also never seen *Easy Rider, Citizen Kane, Duck Soup, Chinatown, Butch Cassidy and the Sundance Kid, Ben Hur, 2001: A Space Odyssey, Sunset Boulevard, Taxi Driver, Some Like It Hot, Roman Holiday, Raging Bull, The Godfather,* or *High Noon.* There are many, many more I could name, but I think you're getting the picture here; I am not a classic movie buff.

I've never seen a movie starring Greta Garbo, Marlene Dietrich, Jane Russell, Jean Harlow, or Grace Kelly. I've been told quite a few times that I resemble Grace Kelly. I know that's a compliment, and I'm flattered. But not flattered enough to actually watch one of her films. There are so many classics I haven't seen that I probably wouldn't have time to catch up at this point. But I decided that I could perhaps turn off the mind-numbing reality crap that has become ubiquitous on television nowadays and pop in a DVD once in a while, at least until I had a few of these gems under my belt.

I started with *Casablanca* for no other reason than it seems to be one of the most quoted movies ever made. I wanted to see for myself what all the fuss was about. The verdict? I didn't get what all the fuss was about. I thought it was good, sure. And of course Ingrid Bergman was beautiful. She looks a lot like her daughter Isabella Rossellini, who I saw in *Cousins*—a cute flick, but certainly not a classic. Okay . . . back to *Casablanca*. War, romance, snappy banter dialogue. Seen it so many times in so many films that unless there's some new twist on it I feel like it's the same old story. Is it possible that *Casablanca* was the first to combine all of those ingredients successfully? If that's the case, then I see why people loved it (and still love it). Maybe my expectations were too high, but it wasn't as good as I'd anticipated, so I gave it a B. One and a half thumbs up, and three and a half stars out of five.

My next pick was *Dr. Zhivago*. I hadn't heard a single thing about this movie except that it was an epic and that there was a lot of snowy scenery. I didn't know who was in it or anything about the plot. You know what else I didn't know? How long the movie was. I didn't bother to check the running time before I pressed play while on a weekend getaway with my husband. We got pretty caught up in this story about Russia, revolution, forbidden love, loss, longing, and more loss. Lots of loss in this one, but it was a really good film. Made in 1965, it starred Omar Sharif and Julie Christie and was rather racy for its day. Rod Steiger was also in it, playing the part of a rough politician who takes advantage of Julie Christie's character. She was seventeen when the story began, and it was implied that she was raped.

When I saw the name "Rod Steiger" on the DVD box, I have to admit I thought it was the name of the actor who played Chief Martin Brody in another classic film I actually *had* seen, *Jaws*. I couldn't for the life of me figure out how the stocky, older, bearded actor who played Victor in *Dr. Zhivago,* could've looked so much younger and thinner *ten years later* in *Jaws*. My husband and I proceeded to argue whether or not Rod Steiger was the drunken shark hunter Quint (which is what my husband thought) or Chief Brody (which is what I thought). Turned out Rod Steiger wasn't even in *Jaws*. The actor in *Jaws* was Roy Scheider and he played Chief Brody, not Quint (Robert Shaw). Even though my hubby and I were both wrong, I was less wrong than he was, and therefore I won the fight (not that I'm keeping track). But I digress.

You know it's a long movie when there's an intermission, as there was in *Zhivago*. Time to stretch, use the bathroom, and get more popcorn. My favorite part about this movie, aside from the intermission, was that the story transcends time. Forbidden love, longing, and loss. You find these themes in a lot of films, past and present, because it works. Worked for me anyway. I gave this one an A–, two thumbs up, and four out of five stars.

I did a little research and found out that Omar Sharif starred in another classic film I'd never seen, *Lawrence of Arabia* (both films were directed by David Lean). I assumed that Sharif played the title character, seeing as how he was Arab and all. But once again, I assumed wrong. That part went to Peter O'Toole. Was Lawrence of Arabia a white guy—an *English* white guy at that? This piqued my interest enough to include *Lawrence of Arabia* in my list of "must-see" classic films.

After checking it out of our local library, I settled in and watched it one evening. Turns out the film was three hours and forty minutes long. That's right, 227 minutes. I had to view it in two sittings. Like I said, Peter O'Toole played the title character, and yes, he is a white guy from England. Actually, he was born in Ireland but was raised in England. Regardless, he isn't from Arabia, and as it turned out, neither was his character. He was taking up the cause of the Arabs in their fight against the Turks. It was unclear to me why the Brits were involved, and I was having a hard time paying attention to the details because I was distracted by O'Toole's good looks and also, of course, Omar Sharif's. I'm not sure I fully understand why Lawrence cracked like he did. Sorry if you haven't seen it. Spoiler Alert! Oops, too late.

Actually, this entire section of the chapter is a spoiler, so if you don't want any details about any of these movies, you might as well just flip to the next section right now. If you're still with me, then I don't mind telling you that I was not thrilled with the ending of *Lawrence of Arabia*. I spent way too much of my time only to be let down by what I considered to be an anticlimactic ending. And so, I gave it a B, one thumb up, and three and a half out of five stars. I did like Omar Sharif in it, though, and so I chose another one of his movies to watch next, *Funny Girl*, which was anything but.

Talk about a misleading title. I know, I know, Barbra Streisand's character, Fanny Brice, was a comedic actress. But Fannie's real life just seemed so sad to me. And Omar's character—what a dunce! I suppose when this movie came out, it was a huge deal for a man if his wife made more money than he did. We've evolved since then, though, so the plot just seemed lame to me. However, the acting was very good. I really enjoyed the musical numbers, both the ones Fannie performed on stage as well as those she performed during her off-stage scenes. There just aren't enough musicals nowadays. Also, I thought Omar Sharif looked as handsome as ever in this film. And I think Barbra Streisand is beautiful, very regal looking. So for her character to keep saying she wasn't pretty or "like the other girls" kind of made me sad for her. I think she was always trying to be funny to cover up her insecurities about her looks. I'd hoped she would have gotten past that by the end, that it would be part of her character's arc, if you will. But I didn't get the impression that she'd changed at all. In fact, she still sang about how she knew she'd "Come back on her knee someday, for whatever my man is, I am his forevermore."

Really Barbra/Fannie? Even if what your man is, is a chauvinistic addict who gambled away your dream house and then resorted to a life of crime so that he wouldn't have to accept help from you? I think what this film needed was a big fat dose of women's lib. That being said, I loved it. And maybe it wasn't a "classic" among classics, but I am glad I took the two hours and fifty-one minutes to watch it. I gave it an A–, one and a half thumbs up, and four out of five stars.

I liked Barbra in *Funny Girl* so much I watched another of her old movies, *The Way We Were*. Robert Redford was definitely that generation's Brad Pitt. He was so gorgeous in this film that I would've watched it even if there were no plot and the acting was terrible. Luckily, neither was true. I had zero expectations when I hit play. The only thing I knew about the film was that Carrie Bradshaw quoted a line from it in an episode of *Sex in the City*, "Your girl is lovely, Hubbell." She said it to Mr. Big when she bumped into him after he'd moved on with some young, gorgeous woman to whom he'd become engaged after having strung Carrie along for what felt like seven hundred seasons of the show. I didn't understand what that meant when Carrie said it, but after I saw *The Way We Were*, I got it.

Once again, love and loss were important themes, both in the film and in the episode of *Sex in the City*, and who can't relate to that? I really liked this movie, and I don't want to give too much away about the story because I hope you will watch it yourself, if you haven't already. I can't be the only person on the planet who missed out on classic films. I gave this one two thumbs up (I'd give it three thumbs if I had three thumbs, because Robert Redford was so amazingly handsome in it), an A+, and five out of five stars.

I realize that my reviews of these classics might not match your own. And frankly, I'm a little concerned with the amount of backlash I'm liable to get just from not loving *Casablanca*. I may not share everyone's opinion of that one, but what I do share, finally, is the experience of having watched it. There are so many great old movies that I never have to waste my time watching mindless garbage ever again. If there's nothing great playing in theaters, or there's not one good thing to watch on my five thousand cable channels (why is that by the way?), then I will rent one of the oldie but goodies from Netflix or Apple TV.

#36 ~~Watch some of the old classic movies (the "must sees" I haven't seen)~~

. . . .

My challenge to try out some things that I'd seen other people enjoy was off to a great start. I found that the classics are considered classics for a reason; namely, that they deal with basic human emotions that are consistent from one generation to the next. I had a feeling that another of the things I wanted to try might be popular for the same reason. Sports have been around since, well, forever, as far as I know. Ancient Greeks and Romans competed in all kinds of athletic contests; although back then they usually ended in someone being eaten by a lion, or something like that. I can't fathom being a spectator of that kind of gore, let alone an aficionado.

I wouldn't have wanted to watch ancient sports, and I've never been remotely interested in watching modern-day sports, either. No, I've never been a big sports fan. I can admit that now because I don't live in Pittsburgh anymore. Pittsburghers bleed black and gold, that's how into sports they are. In fact, I think that if you live in Pittsburgh and you don't root for the Steelers, the Pirates, and the Penguins you get run out of town.

I used to claim my disinterest in sports was a result of having a pipe-smoking, classical-music-loving father. But the truth is, in spite

of my dad's non-jock status, he, like all good Pittsburghers, is a big
fan of all the Pittsburgh teams and so he ditches Rachmaninoff for
Roethlisberger on Sundays during the NFL season. My mother is
also a sports fan. She was pretty athletic herself when she was
younger. She played tennis and golf, taught fencing at summer camp,
and was a very fast runner. Somehow I must have missed that gene.
One time I asked my mom why she never put me in any sports and
she replied, "Well, you never wanted to play. You liked dance. Remember?"

I remember wanting to dance, yes. I did not, however, remember
not wanting to play sports. It's quite possible that had anyone signed
me up for a sport, I might have liked it and even been good at it.
Girls did play sports when I was young, but it wasn't readily encouraged unless the girl asked to play, and I didn't. I only asked for dance
lessons.

I don't know about your school, but a lot of people at mine used
to go to games and cheer for their friends on the various teams. Nobody used to come to dance recitals to cheer on their favorite would-
be ballerinas, not unless they were related to them and under threat
of grounding, anyway. So I never experienced firsthand the phenomenon of fandom, either as a spectator or as a player. When it
came to sports, I just didn't care.

That is a very unpopular way of thinking if you live in Pittsburgh, so I got good at pretending to care. I memorized catch
phrases such as, "The Iron Curtain," "One for the Thumb in '81,"
and "Here Comes the Bus." I even had a "Terrible Towel" tucked
away just in case any true Pittsburgher might come over and de-
mand to see it. And it wasn't too difficult to stay on top of what
sport was in season; the players, coaches, and their associates seemed
to be everywhere. I went to school with Willie Stargell's kids; Lynn
Swan took ballet classes at my dance studio (it wasn't just his last

name that made him a graceful player!); and when I was in elementary school, a well-known football player for the University of Pittsburgh dated a girl who babysat me. Her name was Lisa. His name? Tony Dorsett. He used to come over after my parents left. He was a fun guy—he used to play with us kids and really get us laughing. He did go on to the NFL, but don't ask me what team he was on or what position he played.

Once I left Pittsburgh I stopped feigning interest in sports. When I had kids, though, things changed. I definitely had an interest in the sports they played, what teams they got on, who their coaches were, how the team performed, how much playing time my kids got, etc. I was one of the more vocal moms on the sidelines. Nothing worthy of the seven o'clock news or anything, but I'd say I was pretty involved. Being a *mom* fan and being a *fan* fan, however, are two different things. I was interested as long as I had a kid out there competing, but if it was a professional game, I just couldn't pay attention, let alone cheer anyone on.

Still, I could see that other people had a lot of enthusiasm for their favorite teams. And as I contemplated this challenge, I thought, *hey, I am just as capable of painting my face, waving foam fingers, and drinking beer on weekends as the next gal.* And as long as the lucky chosen team has the good sense to wear uniforms with flattering colors, I could totally see myself wearing team shirts and hats to games. It might be fun now that I don't live in Pittsburgh and am officially off the hook for only rooting for the black and gold. And thank God, because that's a color combo meant only for school buses and bumble bees.

For convenience sake, it would've made sense to choose a team that was geographically desirable so that it would be easy to get to a game. There are two basketball teams, two baseball teams, two soccer teams, and two hockey teams all within the L.A. area. Surprise! I settled on football.

Now I am not one to do things halfway. If I'm going to pick a football team to cheer for, I want it to be one of the best teams out there. "Go hard or go home," right? It was beyond fortuitous that my husband's firm had done business with a media company that owns a magazine that throws a giant Super Bowl party every year. I had the perfect opportunity to begin my journey toward sports fanaticism at the very epicenter of fandom . . . the Super Bowl. Super Bowl XLIV to be exact, The Colts vs. The Saints.

When I got on the plane, I still wasn't sure which team would be lucky enough to have my support, but once I saw all the Saints fans, it was hard not to get swept up in their excitement. The Saints had never won a Super Bowl and had been nicknamed "The Ain'ts." I don't like teasing or bullying of any kind, and so, a feeling started to build in me for this New Orleans team. The feeling was that I wanted them to win. Furthermore, their colors were more like those of the Steelers than the Colts were, and so with the blessing of my Pittsburgh friends, I decided to become a Saints fan.

I'm embarrassed to admit that I was far more excited about the Super Bowl party than I was about the Super Bowl itself. It was going to be a huge crowd at the Raleigh Hotel in Miami: LMFAO would be performing, Jermaine Dupris (that's Janet Jackson's ex) would DJ, and, of course, there would be a red carpet and lots of celebrities. Maybe not A-list celebrities, but celebrities just the same. The party was outside, they'd completely transformed the property for the event, and the weather was Miami mild. It was absolutely the coolest party I'd ever attended.

Now that I've gotten that out of the way, let me tell you about the football game. When I saw all the Saints fans wearing Mardi Gras beads, I knew I'd picked the right team to root for. Who wouldn't want to be a Saints fan? I would tell you about the game itself, but I don't remember anything about it. I was paying attention, and at the time I followed the action: I took cues from the fans all around me as to when to jump up and cheer and when to smack my knee and curse the refs or the Colts. There were far fewer Colts fans at the game than there were Saints fans; either that or Saints fans are just extra loud. It was easy to see how passionate and emotionally invested the Saints fans were in this game.

I was feeling passionate and emotionally invested, too, for every aspect of this underdog story, except the actual playing of the football game. I loved lending my voice to the loyal fans', willing the Saints to a victory. I didn't love watching the game; I loved the drama surrounding the game. I suppose I can't say that I was completely successful in my goal to become a sports fan if by definition, it required being a fan of the sport and not just a fan of being a fan. Regardless, I had a great time and enjoyed the added bonus of making just about everyone jealous that I got to witness *in person*, the Ain'ts become the Saints once more.

That included the teller at the bank. When I told her I'd been at the Super Bowl she was duly impressed. She was not impressed, however, with the half-time show. "The Who . . . I mean, who *are* they exactly?" WHAT? Was I hearing her right? It wasn't that she didn't like them, she just didn't know who they were?

"Who *are* they? They're The Who, that's who! You know their music, I'm sure you do. Even if you don't think you do, you do." I was being a bit forceful as if by convincing the teller that she actually did know The Who, I'd be convincing myself that I wasn't ancient. But then I realized, it was just like everything else; a matter of taste. Her not loving The Who was the equivalent of me not loving football. Her not really being familiar with their music was like me not having seen famous old movies.

"Download a few of their songs from iTunes," I suggested to her. "Give them a chance. You might really like them, a lot of people do." I felt like I'd just given her some very good advice. Not just about music, but about life in general. Popular things are popular for a reason, and so it makes sense to try things so you can decide for yourself whether they're for you or not.

#37 ~~Be a sports fan~~

. . . .

In my next challenge, I went from watching sports to participating in one. Paddle boarding was something that I'd seen someone do with great enthusiasm, and that someone was Cameron Diaz. Yes, I'd seen photos in *People* magazine, no doubt taken by paparazzi, of Cameron on vacation paddle boarding like a champion. I was impressed with both her athletic ability and her ability to keep her white string bikini on while paddling through the waves on what appeared to be a surfboard. I decided I wanted to try it myself, minus the waves (remember the surfing incident), and minus the bikini. I would have my first lesson in a calm bay wearing a tank top and shorts.

I was in San Diego visiting my mom and her girlfriend Suzanne, who is a great paddle boarder. She had offered to take me out after I let it drop casually that it was one of my challenges. We strapped two boards on the roof of her Prius and headed down to Mission Bay. I was feeling pretty confident that I would be a good paddle boarder. I had all the necessary ingredients; strong legs and core, and a low center of gravity (one of the few advantages of being short). Unfortunately, those ingredients disintegrate in water.

When I got on the board I looked less like Cameron Diaz and more like Shaky the Clown. The board was shaking like crazy. I thought it was the board, but when I looked down I saw that it was my legs. The more I looked at them, the more they shook. I finally looked up to see where my board was heading and when I did, the shaking stopped. I remembered the oar in my hands and started paddling, following Suzanne's lead. I paddled on the left, and on the right, and propelled myself around the bay. Once I got the hang of it, I had a blast.

In addition to paddle boarding, Suzanne is an excellent photographer and she'd brought along her waterproof camera. I decided it would be a great idea to have a photo my first paddle boarding experience. But the second I turned around and struck my best Cameron Diaz-like pose, Shaky the Clown came back, and down I went. It was not pretty. It was not graceful. But it was funnier than hell, and it was documented for all eternity on film.

I climbed right back on my board, my shorts and tank top completely drenched, and managed to stand up right away. I wasn't about to let Shaky the Clown get the best of me. Suzanne got to shore before me and I heard her call out excitedly to my mother as I drifted in shivering and drenched, "Did you see her fall?!" She had, and much laughter ensued. I started to feel angry. I wanted to defend myself and point out that I had only fallen once, and I got right back on my board. But then I asked myself, WWCDD (What would Cameron Diaz do)? Probably she'd laugh at herself and brush it off. And so I decided I would, too.

I realized later how much I'd grown since I started living my list. The old me wouldn't have tried paddle boarding in the first place. But if she had, and if she fell, she would have let that wreck the whole experience for her. She would have felt humiliated and defeated and she definitely would have felt the sting of being laughed at, especially by her own mother. The new and improved me? Well she may not be Cameron Diaz, but she's still pretty awesome.

#38 ~~Go paddle boarding~~

. . . .

When you are making your list, don't hesitate to include some of the things that you've noticed other people enjoying, but that you, yourself, have never tried. You may find out you were right to have steered clear all this time, or you may just find a new passion or pastime. Either way, you'll have an educated opinion of said activity, instead of just wondering what all the fuss is about.

TWELVE

I AM WHAT I AM

Popeye sure knew what he was talking about when he said, "I am what I am." Self-awareness and self-acceptance turned out to be the true themes of my journey, although I certainly didn't know it when I first made my list. My midlife flip-out was all about the things I hadn't done, and I thought that somehow in doing them, I was going to be magically changed into someone else. But my experiences didn't change me. They changed how I saw myself, and how I felt about myself. In the end I wasn't different, I was simply *more* me. I now know it's impossible to be anyone other than who I am, and, more important, I don't want to.

Two goals that really helped me finally embrace that "I am what I am" philosophy were "go au naturel for a week," and the last challenge on my list, #40, "write a book." Both were about acknowledging, accepting, and embracing who I am—inside and out.

. . . .

Forgoing all embellishments to my appearance—or as I like to call it, going au naturel—wasn't the most difficult goal on my list. But for me, it was one of the most challenging. Before you laugh, let me ask a few questions to any middle-age women who are reading this right now. Are you currently sporting your natural hair color? How comfortable are you being seen in public without any makeup (not even powder or lip gloss)? Do you wear high heels? How about self tanner in the winter? There are a million ways in which we modify our appearance. For me it was like putting on a disguise of sorts; I was trying to look like someone other than myself. What was I saying to the world by doing this? What message was I sending to myself? That I was not beautiful just as I was? I thought back to when I first started making alterations to my appearance, and why I had done it.

The year was 1983. Reagan was president. *Flashdance* ruled the box office, not to mention my wardrobe. "Hungry Like the Wolf," "C'mon Eileen," and "You Can't Hurry Love" were popular songs on the radio. I made quite a few life changing discoveries my eigth-grade year, not the least of which was a cheap, peroxide-based, spray-in hair lightener called *Sun In*. It left my locks dry, frizzy, and orange. It looked terrible, of course, but the mere fact that it was different than my natural color made it a vast improvement in my opinion. I had decided long ago that my hair color was unacceptable. It was not dark enough for me to be considered a brunette and not light enough to qualify me as a blonde. I was stuck in the middle, and I hated it. It was nondescript. Proof that it was utterly unmemorable? I myself could not remember it, which made my task of returning to my roots for my quest to go au naturel more than a little bit challenging.

I looked at the photos of me as a little girl—there aren't that many of them—and my hair appeared to be light brown with natural dark honey and auburn highlights. It was actually very nice. I wondered why I had hated it so much that I would have started coloring it in the first place. After giving it some thought, all I could come up with was this: It wasn't the same as my sister's.

Elizabeth is three years and three months older than I am. This age spread doomed me to never be happy with myself. It's nobody's fault, least of all Elizabeth's, it just was an unfortunate effect of her always getting whatever it was I wanted, right when discovered I wanted it. I'll break it down. When I was ten, I, like most ten-year-old girls, wanted to be a teenager. How old was Elizabeth? Thirteen. When I was finally thirteen, I wanted to be what most thirteen-year-old girls wanted to be, sweet sixteen. I don't need to tell you how old Elizabeth was, I'm sure you can do the math. Of course when I was sixteen, I wanted to be off at college and independent. I was always envious of what Elizabeth had, even when I was two. That was when I first realized that she had straight blonde hair, and I did not.

So one day I took a big pair of scissors out of my mother's sewing basket and cut every last brown curl off of my head. As soon as Elizabeth saw what I'd done she ran off to tattle on me. I realized I was going to be in big trouble, and tried to tape my hair back on. This, of course, resulted in my being shorn nearly bald in order to free my head from the wads of sticky tape. After all was said and done, I didn't look any more like my sister. I looked like a mini Marine. My mother was so happy when my hair started growing back that she didn't cut it again until I was six. By then my sister Elizabeth's hair had darkened to a shade she always referred to as "dishwater blond" which to me, still sounded better than my own "mouse brown."

Sun In was my first attempt to change it, but it certainly was not my last. Over the years I've had just about every shade of brown (other than my own self-deemed unacceptable shade that is), blond, and one time, almost black. "Elvira" was not the look I was going for (but was what I ended up with). That dye-job debacle occurred right before my grandmother's one-hundredth birthday party, and I cringe every time I see the photos.

For years after that I continued to change my color regularly before finally settling on a dark-blond shade that was achieved by highlighting. I stopped using allover color, and so, in time, what I was left with was my own base color, and the blonde highlights. It took years for me to get there, but once I did, for first time in my life, I actually liked my hair. And so, for several years prior to my list making, I had it just that way. It was difficult for me to bite the bullet and hide those highlights under a wash of light brown in my efforts to duplicate my natural hue. But I knew it was only a matter of time before I'd start getting some grays and want to color over my base, thus losing, forever, my ability to match it. If I ever wanted to experience what it would be like to just have the hair God gave me, (or as close as I could get to it with a professional dye job) it was now or never.

I should have taken a picture of my colorist's face when I asked him to color over the highlights he'd so carefully painted in. I'd brought along some pictures I'd pulled out of magazines so he could get an idea of the color I wanted him to match. "Can you do this?" I asked.

"Of course I can do that. I can do anything," He said. "The question is why on earth would you want me to?" I tried explaining to him about how I wanted to go back to my natural color, just to see if I felt more like me. "Well, you are a blonde," he said, matter-of-factly.

"You should know better than anyone that I'm not." Where was he going with this?

"I know your hair isn't blond. But *you* are blonde. To me, that's how you should be, and that's how I see you, and that's why your hair looks so great when I do it." I sensed this was a compliment to himself, albeit well deserved (the man is a genius with color), and he may very well have been right. But I was the customer, and I'd asked for light brown. Light brown was what I wanted. Light brown was what I was paying for. Light brown was what I should get.

"Okay," he sighed, "but I'm only doing a semipermanent color wash. You aren't going to want to keep it, and this way, it'll be easier on me when you come back here next month wanting me to make you blond again." Maybe I should have been offended, but to be honest, I was relieved that I wouldn't be stuck if it turned out he was right and I did indeed hate the light brown color.

About an hour later, I took a look at the new, old, me. It was a perfectly fine shade of light golden brown. I looked like a grown-up version of my little girl self. That was the last time I'd seen myself with this color. It was kind of odd, like my hair was my young hair, but my face was my same old face. It wasn't bad, but it would take some getting used to.

After my hair appointment I stopped in a little café to get a bite to eat. It may have been my imagination, but I was not getting a whole lot of attention. Normally, people make eye contact, smile, or even strike up a conversation when I am somewhere alone. Not today. Maybe I'm crazy, but I think it might have been my hair. Was I blending into the scenery? Later that day I saw my mother. She said she liked my hair that way, and that yes, it was the color she remembered my hair to be when I was young. "It looks good. You look pretty. It's a lot less *Hollywood*." She probably meant that as a compliment. I think.

My hair color was not the only thing that I'd spent years trying to change about myself. I am short, so I wear high heels almost every day. Sure my feet hurt and I'll probably end up developing bunions, but those few extra inches are worth it. I even have shoes that, from the front, look like regular loafers that any suburban mom would wear. You would never guess that hidden by the length of my pants, is a three-inch wedge heel. I call them my mullet shoes because just like a mullet, they are business up front, party in the back. I wear them to auditions. (Getting a paid acting job was something on my list that I enjoyed enough to keep on doing.) Over time I've learned a few tricks of the trade. My mom-like "flat" loafers were for auditions where I needed to look casual, and taller, at the same time.

Another wardrobe trick I picked up from my newfound acting career was SPANX. If you aren't familiar with this miracle of illusion, SPANX are basically a modern-day version of the girdle your dear old granny used to wear, only thanks to modern technology, much, much, stronger. The first time I ever tried on a pair it was at the request of a wardrobe stylist on the set of a commercial shoot. I was simultaneously intrigued and insulted. "I need SPANX?" I said to her. I realized my midsection wasn't quite as firm as it had been prior to having three babies, but did I really need a girdle?

"Don't worry honey," the stylist said, handing me a pair, "I even put them on my double zeros. If SPANX weren't for everybody, they wouldn't come in extra small." Reluctantly, I pulled them on, and I must say, I was impressed with how well they smoothed out the muffin top that was rising over my jeans. I imagined they were a whole lot cheaper than liposuction, although perhaps only a smidge less uncomfortable. After that shoot I went straight out and bought three pair.

Another thing I've been able to alter about myself is my skin tone. I am fair. In Los Angeles, that makes me stick out like a sore thumb—a sore, pasty white, thumb. So, I slather up with self-tanner and brush on powdered bronzer, and before special events, I get airbrushed (aka spray-tanned). Yes, in order to have tan skin, I willingly subject myself to the humiliation of standing buck naked *under fluorescent lights*, in front of a stranger wielding a metal spray gun full of seriously freezing and smelly mist, most likely laced with chemicals I cannot pronounce, and do not want to know the side effects of. This procedure lasts about fifteen minutes, but I can't shower or wash my hands for eight sticky hours. I gladly pay an arm and a leg for this all-day torture fest, just so I can sport a faux glow that lasts about a week.

On top of all the aforementioned self-alterations, I also ditched my makeup bag. I am one of those women who likes to put on at least a swipe of mascara and lip gloss before I walk to my mailbox, so this was not easy. Also, my issues with my hair aren't limited to color; the texture, which is naturally curly/wavy/frizzy, is problematic (in my mind, at least) as well. Once, when I was in college, a new stylist told me my curl was erotic. I must have turned three shades of red as I thanked him for the compliment, but then I turned three more shades when he corrected me. *Erotic* does sound a lot like *erratic*. Simple mistake. Since then I've tried just about every contraption and concoction on the market to tame my mane. But, for one week, I was going to have to embrace my inner poodle. Insert dog joke here.

Believe me, I was dreading going around looking like that, and by that, I mean like myself. I just wanted to know what it felt like to do so, however. Would it change the way people treated me? Would it change the way I felt about myself? Would it make me feel shy? Or would it be liberating? Would I feel less like myself if I looked more like myself? Would stripping away my external lies help me to discover some internal truths? I had hoped that by removing these outward layers of fakeness that I would feel more empowered, and more me. But that's not what happened at all. Instead of feeling like I'd taken off a costume, I felt like I had put one on. I could almost hear myself being announced before entering every room, "The role of Mouse Girl will now be played by Susan Campbell Cross." And I acted every bit the part, too.

Why it is that I associate pale skin, light brown hair, no makeup, and flats with a mousey disposition? Hmmm . . . could it be the influence of modern media? Probably. I'm not an expert on sociology.

What I do know is that after living with my new/old look for a week, I realized that while I really wanted to feel just as pretty without all that stuff, I simply did not. And that's perfectly okay.

I look at these outward modifications as a form of expressing my inner self. Maybe I'm more comfortable in heels than flats because I like the lift they give me. And I like having a little glow to my skin; when I look radiant, I *feel* radiant. And as for my hair, well, maybe my hair guru had it right all along. I may not be blond, but gosh darn it, I *am* a blonde—at least for now. I love that I can change things about my appearance. Why the heck not? None of the things I do is permanent, clearly, and if it's going to make me feel more like myself, then why not? People change their clothes every day, and what we wear reflects how we feel.

I think going forward I will look at all changeable aspects of my appearance the same way. If it's something that's easily undone, or redone, then I'm going to let my outer look reflect my inner attitude. I will change it up as I see fit, and as often as I see fit, and not because I think I'm not good enough without all that stuff, I know I'm good enough without it. I just happen to like the way I look better with it, and liking the way I look makes me feel happy and confident. And that's what I am.

#39 Go au naturel for a week

. . . .

My Grandma Joan was a child of the Great Depression. She saved everything, including scraps of wrapping paper, ribbon, and fabric, which she'd let us grandkids have for art projects. I used those things to make books. I would write a story on paper and make covers out of the recycled craft supplies. There was one titled *Childron and Parints* that I wrote when I was five (that explains the spelling), which was about a little girl who got lost in a department store. It was a simple story, but it had all the key elements: a protagonist, a plot, a conflict, a setting, and a theme. My grandmother saved it for years, and I remember her pulling it out and showing it to her friends sometimes and bragging about how smart and creative I was. My mom recently gave that little book to me, and I consider it one of my most valuable possessions. It's evidence of an indisputable truth about myself. I am a writer.

Even though I've known this all along, I never felt comfortable saying it out loud until now. Maybe that's because I never wrote anything that I let anyone read until now, aside from advertising copy and papers for school. I would occasionally write a short story that would sit on my computer desktop, and one time I took a stab at writing a screenplay. I had an idea for a film inspired by the events surrounding my sister's car accident and recovery. I went so far as to purchase Syd Field's *Final Draft* screenwriting software and instructional video.

I got pretty far into it and had the concept all worked out in my mind: I remember explaining to someone at a party how one character was really the ghost of someone who the main character had known in high school, a really meaty part that I envisioned someone like Wesley Snipes playing. Then, as if there had a been a movie about me writing a movie, it turned out the person I was talking to worked for Wesley Snipes and was responsible for reading scripts that were sent his way. She thought it might be a great fit, and she told me to send it along as soon as I was finished.

As if on cue, that little voice in my head piped in. *What if* I write the screenplay and Wesley Snipes hates it? *What if* I write the screenplay and Wesley Snipes loves it, but then everybody expects me to write more great screenplays, and the next one sucks? The stars had aligned, lighting a path toward a dream, and I turned around and ran the other way. I was afraid to fail *and* afraid to succeed. I was afraid period. I came up with an excuse as to why I didn't finish the screenplay, but the real reason was fear. The true F-bomb is revealed.

I used to think it was forty. Now that I'm on the other side of that number, though, I realize that's all it ever was: a number. Yes, fear was the real enemy. I spent years of my life denying that fact, putting my dreams on hold and blaming it on any number of things. I had quite an arsenal of colorful and varied excuses. Here are a few of my favorites—see if any of them sound familiar to you.

- I can't take time away from my family because it would be selfish.
- If I do blankety blank, I might get hurt, and then who would take care of everybody?
- I don't want to spend money on myself that should be saved for the kids.
- What would people think of me if I did blankety blank?
- If I do blankety blank, and fail at it, what will that say about me?
- I already know I'd suck at blankety blank. I don't need to prove it to myself.

For every one of these excuses, there is an underlying fear. The fear of failing and the fear of succeeding were just the tip of the iceberg. I had quite a collection of different fears, including the fear of rejection, the fear of being judged, the fear of being hurt physically, the fear of being hurt emotionally, the fear of causing someone else to be hurt physically or emotionally. I also had some of the garden-variety phobias, including fear of crashing, fear of falling, fear of drowning, and fear of enclosed spaces. Regardless of what form the fear takes, it's still a fear, and therefore it comes from the same emotional origin.

Fear was the single reason I hadn't done any of the things on my list sooner. It was the poison that rendered me paralyzed. Accepting this and learning how to deal with it head-on, was what ultimately led me to discover the antidote, love. Just as I had a lot of different fears, I had a lot of different loves. These loves were the motivation behind my chosen activities: love of adventure, love of performing, love of freedom, love of the ocean, love of my children. But the one love that I absolutely had to have in order to take on those challenges was the love of self. I had to love myself and treat myself accordingly. That is how I was able to work through my fears and achieve my forty goals.

And so with this last chapter I have come to the end of my list. #40 was "write a book." Yes, "write a book" was the last thing on my list. Not because it was the least important, quite the opposite really. Writing this book was the *most* important thing I wanted to achieve. When I write, my true self is exposed, and I am at my most vulnerable. It is my way of letting people in, and once they're in, I am wide open to criticism. I was afraid that nobody would read it, and simultaneously afraid that everybody would read it but nobody would relate to it. I was afraid people wouldn't like what I had to say. I was afraid people wouldn't like the way I said it. I was afraid people wouldn't like *me*. And so, writing this book was by far the scariest of all the challenges on my list. I wrote it anyway.

All those fears I mentioned were based on what I imagined other people might think of me. But I wasn't writing the book for them. I was writing it for myself. And since my goal was "write a book," it would be accomplished even if nobody read it. And if everybody read it but nobody related to it and nobody liked what I had to say, then they could all just read something else. And if they didn't like me, well, after all I'd been through accomplishing #1 through #39, I learned something really, really, important. *I* like me. And that's all that really matters. If someone else likes me, too, that's nice, but not necessary. I put that last goal on my list because of my love of writing. In the end I couldn't come up with a single fear that couldn't be squelched with the love I now had for myself.

The riskiest endeavors are often the most rewarding. What I gained from achieving my goal was so much more than a sense of accomplishment. I gained a sense of self and a sense of purpose. I am what I am, and I realized that what I am is a writer, a communicator of ideas and thoughts, and a teller of tales.

Before I began my journey, I thought I was the only person who felt like something was missing. That couldn't have been further from the truth. Other people who have heard my story have related to it, *a lot*. Turns out, I'm not the only one in the world who ever put her life on hold. I'm not the only person who ever let fear keep her from pursuing her dreams and fulfilling her potential.

I never tire of talking about how this list changed my life, and I never tire of seeing that lightbulb go off above peoples' heads when they realize that this is something anybody can (and should) do. In fact, many people have started lists of their own. I've received some amazing e-mails from individuals who've shared their adventures with me and thanked me for having inspired them to go for it. There is a woman somewhere in the world right now who is playing the harmonica because of me. Another is studying acting, and another is taking voice lessons. Another went back to school and became a medical assistant, and another is writing a book of her own. It is an awesome and humbling feeling to know that because I went after my dreams, thousands of other people will, too. It is my sincere hope that you will be one of them.

Don't wait until you have a crisis, midlife or otherwise, to re-evaluate your life. Start today. There's no expiration date on dreams, and there's no such thing as too old, or too late. And so, I hereby challenge you to get a pen and paper, set some time aside, and start making a list of your own. You can include anything you want. Don't worry if some of the things you come up with seem a little crazy. Write them down anyway, and then start doing them. When you do, you will begin to really live your life—and to love it, too. When you've crossed off the last challenge, make a new list. That's what I'm going to do right now.

#40 ~~Write a book~~

EPILOGUE

I hope you were as inspired reading this book as I was writing it. Just in case you aren't completely convinced that a list can change your life, I wanted to share a little of what's been happening in mine. Looking back now, I think it's funny that I ever thought that writing this book was the culmination of a long journey. It really was just the beginning of one. Remember that chapter about how one thing leads to another? That phenomenon keeps on happening!

When the book was finished, I sent some sample chapters to a few contacts in media, not really knowing what would come of it. I was hoping for feedback and advice on how one goes about getting a book published. I got that, and so much more. Remember my fears that people might not like the book, my writing, my message, or me? None of those things happened. Here's what did. A number of magazines ran articles about my life-changing adventure, and then I started getting offers to write about it myself. Now I'm writing life-style articles for several national publications and online sites. Through my "get a paid acting job" challenge and subsequent gig as a commercial actor, I've become pretty comfortable on camera, and I'm starting to do lifestyle segments on TV.

Every time someone introduces me as a "lifestyle expert" I can't help but giggle just a bit. It wasn't too long ago that I felt like my own life was devoid of style, at least any sort of style that reflected who I was as an individual. I'm always quick to point out that I don't have a degree in psychology and I'm not a certified life coach—or a certified anything else, for that matter. What I am is someone who's been through a lot and not just willing but *thrilled* to share what she's learned. So yes, I suppose when it comes to lifestyle—or more accurately re-styling your life, I have indeed become an expert. This book is done, but my journey continues. I don't know how or where it will end, but of this I am certain: It started with a list.

ACKNOWLEDGMENTS

Writing this book was quite a journey and if I could list every one of my travel companions by name, I would. If you aren't mentioned here, please know that your contribution is deeply appreciated.

To the team at February Books, your dedication to this project has been tireless and steadfast. To Gretchen Crary and Dee Dee De Bartlo in particular: I owe you a debt of gratitude for your unwavering belief in this book and in me. A special thank you to Anne Cole Norman for her kind and encouraging words and gentle edits.

I am blessed to have many dear friends (you know who you are!) who inspire and encourage me in all endeavors. You make my life sweeter, richer, and so much fun!

I hope my parents know how big an influence they are in my life. Thank you for everything you've ever done for me—I am who I am because of you and for that I am forever grateful.

To my amazing husband Keven: Your love, understanding, support, and seemingly endless supply of patience made it possible for me to achieve the balance that was essential to realizing my dreams.

And finally to my beautiful children, Kayla, Rory, and Aidan: you have a permanent spot at the very top of my list and being your mother will always be the greatest, most joyful adventure of all.